Dan Leno, His Book: A Volume Of Frivolities Autobiographical, Historical, Philosophical, Anecdotal, And Nonsensical

Dan Leno

DAN LENO

HYS BOOKE

WRITTEN BY

HIMSELF

DAN LENO
Hys Booke ~

Written by
Himself

A Volume of Frivolities

AUTOBIOGRAPHICAL, HISTORICAL, PHILOSOPHICAL
ANECDOTAL, AND NONSENSICAL

Illustrated by

S. H. SIME, ALFRED BRYAN, FRANK CHESWORTH
W. S. ROGERS, GUSTAVE DARRÉ
THE AUTHOR
AND SEVERAL PHOTOGRAPHERS

THIRD EDITION

WITH AN APPRECIATION OF THE AUTHOR BY
CLEMENT SCOTT

LONDON
GREENING & CO.
20, CECIL COURT, CHARING CROSS ROAD, W.C.
1899

Galvin, George

𝕿his little 𝖁olume

IS RESPECTFULLY DEDICATED

TO

MY FRIENDS IN FRONT

FROM THE

FIRST ROW OF STALLS

TO THE

GALLERY BAR

Dan Leno

HIMSELF.

CONTENTS

List of Illustrations

The sketches by S. H. Sime on pages 43 and 101 are reproduced by permission of the proprietors of *Pick-Me-Up*. Those by the same artist on pages 19 and 98 by permission of the proprietor of *The Favorite* magazine. The drawings by Alfred Bryan, on the cover and pages 113, 127, and 139, are by permission of the proprietor of *The Entracte*; and the sketch by Frank Chesworth on page 63 is reproduced by permission of the proprietors of *Illustrated Bits*.

The bust of the author on page 135 is reproduced from *The Dramatic World*.

The publishers desire to thank the above-mentioned proprietors for their courtesy.

Introductory

ENTRE NOUS.

THEY say that the pen is mightier than the sword, but I doubt it; for even in times of peace a sword may come in handy for chopping wood or carving an autumn chicken, and you can't do much in that line with a pen without crossing the nib. However, what I can do with a pen is now on sale; and, looking through it again, I am most struck by the number of things I have omitted which might have left the world wiser than they found it; so that as soon as I had finished I felt like starting to write another volume. My friends succeeded in restraining me for the moment; but I feel I ought to give the public a short account of my pantomime experiences, my sporting and athletic adventures, &c.—above all, how I discovered America. And if I make enough out of this first book to enable me to retire from the stage, and devote myself to literature for the remainder of my life, I do not see why I should not write a book every year.

B

Dan Leno : An Impression

By CLEMENT SCOTT

DURING the best part of the last half century I have seen all the best, the drollest, the most pathetic and tragic comedians, whose humour, variety, tenderness, and intensity have delighted the playgoers of the world. Amongst these representatives of art and sometimes genius, Dan Leno holds his own bravely indeed. Nay, I am not sure that in certain gifts of expression, variety, and, if I may so express it, tornado of instant comic farce, Dan Leno has ever had a rival. You may probably ask me what I mean by a pathetic low comedian and a tragic low comedian? What I mean is this—that the border line between pathos and humour, between tragedy and comedy, is extremely small. There are certain low comedians who owe their success to nature. Their faces are their fortune. They have nothing to do but to come on, and smile, or talk, to set the house on a roar. But when to nature art is added, then we are on the confines of genius.

Take Robson, for instance, perhaps the most admirable comedian I have ever seen. I can roar now to myself with recollections of him in the "Boots at the Swan," and yet this same little ball of fun could, in his burlesque of "Medea and Shylock," come within half an inch of tragedy. He had electric bursts that were astonishing, and he held the house in a vice as Edmund Kean must have done. Take again John S. Clarke, one of the very drollest comedians I have ever seen, as I could prove by pointing to his "Toodles" and "Dr. Pangloss" and "Bob Acres." But for all that, his comedy had the force and intensity of tragedy, and he has acted to me scenes from "Richard the Third" and bits from "Sir Giles Overreach" with startling nervous force, showing that he was within measurable distance of a tragedian. The pathetic comedian was best represented by Jimmy Rogers, of the Strand, and Johnnie Toole. The humour of Rogers was gentle and exquisitely pathetic, whilst Johnnie Toole, who for countless years has healed our grief with honest laughter, has in such characters as "Caleb Plummer" and "Stephen Digges" flooded the theatre with tears. And who shall forget the jovial, genial Buckstone, of the Haymarket, who made the house laugh directly his voice was heard behind the scenes; the grim, formal, and pedantic Compton, the best of all Shakespearean clowns; the inimitable Geoffroy and the unctuous-voiced Daubray, and the quaint Ravel, of France, down to our own latter-day Arthur Roberts, quick as lightning, alert, a spark of comic electricity, and Penley, the prince of drollery?

With these great representatives of comedy Dan Leno need not fear comparison. In petticoats, and as a representative of various women of the lodging-house and slavey class, he would have beaten Jimmy Rogers at his own game. When we see Dan Leno as a woman, and hear his delightful patter, it never strikes us that it is a man imitating a woman. It is a woman who stands before us, the veritable Mrs. Kelly, not a burlesque of the sex, but the actual thing. He catches every expression, every trick, every attitude, every inflexion of voice, and all is done without offence or a suspicion of vulgarity. In his grim earnestness consists his humour. The comedian who laughs at his own jokes soon becomes wearisome, but it is Dan Leno's astonished face when he looks at the laughing audience that gives him his power. In brief, a most admirable, versatile, persuasive, volatile, and intense comedian and artist. Whenever he is on the stage, be it theatre or music-hall, he literally holds his audience tight in his power. They cannot get away from him. He is monarch of all he surveys.

Long then may the reign of King Dan Leno last; long may he be spared to us, to delight the children at pantomime time, and to make those who, though going downhill, are not ashamed to laugh, as young, at least in heart, as the little ones by their side.

DAN LENO
Hys Booke

CHAPTER FIRST

How I Was Born

I CAME into the world a mere child, without a rag to my back and without a penny in my pocket, and now I am a farthing millionaire. I have a town house in the most fashionable part of the suburbs of Brixton, and an acre and two pints of some of the best wasp-stalking in the kingdom.

You know, although I have to spend a lot of time in London, I am at home in the country amongst my wasps. I love to sit between my cows at milking time, when I'm thirsty, and it's too far to go and get a drink anywhere else. You see, mine are not ordinary cows. One of them is just a plain unadulterated milk cow, with a little cream on it, but no froth; but the other is not exactly a milk cow: *it's* a rum cow—one of the rummest cows——

But I'm going to tell you all about my country pleasures in another chapter. I have to be born first.

Everybody—mark this—everybody has to be born one way or the other. There's no getting away from it. You have to go through this inconvenience. You can't say you just happened to be passing, and you dropped in to see how mother's getting on. No!

The fact is, I simply revel in country sports. You won't expect me to say that I like my professional work. Don't press me. If I said that they would want me to pay for going on. I should turn up at the Canterbury one night, and they would say—

"Oh, we've heard all about you! Why, you like work. You're not coming in here for less than five pounds a night to enjoy your little treat."

And when the shareholders' meetings came round the directors would say that the increased dividend was due to the fact that Mr. Dan Leno had been very fond of appearing during this year, and they had been able to charge him a higher salary.

No, no! I don't give myself away like that. I'm going to keep on being paid, and then, in about thirty or forty years, I shall be able to retire on a small incompetency.

But still I'm waiting to be born, while I'm running on with this incoherent patter.

DAN LENO AT HOME.

It was about five minutes past one in the morning, Piccadilly time——

One moment! I do hope you don't think I'm egotistical in coming out of my shell, so to speak, and writing a book about myself, because if you do, I'll chuck it. It hurts me just as much as it does you.

To resume—

I was annoyed when I saw the way they treated me. Instead of turning me over and over, and upside down, and playing lawn tennis with me on the bed-quilt, I think father might at least have lent me a pair of trousers to go on with.

"It seems to me," I said sternly to my dad—of course I'm giving you a free translation, they didn't understand my dialect—"it seems to me, old man, we've had about enough of this knock-about business. There is nothing exceptional about this affair. Birth comes to all sooner or later. Let's talk this matter over as between one man of the world and another. If you're prepared to set me on my legs and let me come in on sharing terms, well and good; if not, off I go. Understand that I'm here to do business, not to be heaved about."

But will you believe me when I tell you that it was some years before I could get people to understand what I was talking about. They had to be educated up to me.

That was in the year 1861, on the 32nd of Danuary, and it occurred in Eve Court, King's

Cross, London. London is a large village on the Thames, where the principal industries carried on are music-halls and the confidence trick. It is a curious fact that the place where I was born is now covered over by St. Pancras Station, and it's rather aggravating to know that somewhere underneath that station there's a little property belonging to me that I can't get at. Once, when I was in a meditative mood, I went to the main line departure platform, and mused.

"Here," I said to myself, with my hand buried in my brows, "here I was born. Ah!——"

"By your leave," shouted a porter.

"I wasn't asked," I told him; and then I came back to myself out of my muse, and disentangled myself from a pile of trunks and bags and bicycles just as I was being shot into the luggage van with a label dabbed on my nose. How is a man to muse when he's suddenly scooped up into a porter's barrow?

But I had another try.

"Here"—you generally begin with "Here"— "here I spent my happy childhood hours. Ah! what is man? Wherefore does he why? Whence did he whence? Whither is he withering?"

Then the guard yelled out: "Leicester, Derby, Nottingham, Manchester, Liverpool!"

And that sort of thing makes a man feel a bit pessimistic. It does not satisfy the yearnings of his inwards.

Even then I went on with my soliloquy. I was

not going to be beaten. I took off my coat, rolled up my shirt sleeves, and mused some more.

But just as I made a dignified gesture with my right arm and murmured, "What are we here for? Is life all full of emptiness?" an old lady put twopence in my hand, and asked me if that was the train for the Isle of Wight.

So I decided to let my birthplace alone for that year. And on my next birthday I got connected with it by telephone, and mused through that.

I said—you know how you get snappy at the telephone—"Are you there? D'year? Are you there? What is man?"

"Who are you?" yelled the man at St. Pancras.

"Who am I?" I said in a sad voice; "ah! who is any of us?"

"Eh! what is it you want?"

"'Tis now thirty-five long, short, weary years ago," I soliloquised with my mouth against the box, "since I first came into the world."

"We didn't ring you up," said the man at the other end; "there must be some mistake."

That makes me a little irritated.

"Aren't you St. Pancras?" I demand.

"Yes."

"Very well then, you're covering up my birth-place, and I want to make some philosophical anniversary remarks. Why can't you go away instead of interrupting me when I'm musing with your insulting questions? What? Who's that? Miss Exchange? What have you cut me off Mr.

Pancras for? Oh! did they? Said it wasn't a solilophone, did they? Well, but solilograms cost a halfpenny a word. Think they would? Let me send it cheaper as it's my birthday? Oh, don't go!"

But she does go, and I put the soliloquery shutters up.

There is one thing in connection with my birth that I think I ought to put right, and that is the great fire which broke out in London on that evening. I want to make it quite clear that I had nothing whatever to do with it. I might have been the excuse for the fire, but I was not the cause; and I know for a fact that there have been several fires since then.

I am sorry to say that I have a very indistinct recollection of my early childhood; I only remember that I had a longing to chew everything within reach, more especially lucifer matches and kid gloves. And I remember that I very soon displayed artistic ability, for having procured a large quantity of strawberry jam I varnished all the furniture of a room with it, including the exterior of the cat and the interior of a pair of my dad's new boots, which he declared went on more easily next time he tried them. The cat had no taste for strawberry jam, and only washed itself at the rate of about two square inches a day.

Now that I am born I will describe some of my other adventures.

CHAPTER
SECOND

My First Appearance in Public

IT was after I was born. I was three years old
just at the moment, and I had not quite
finished my education. Well, this is what they
did to me. They put me on a pair of stockings
and nothing else ; ladies' stockings they were (I
blushed, I can tell you), and one was red and the
other blue. Then, when they had put the stockings
on, they fastened them round my neck with a
garter, and I was ready.

I cannot claim that I obtained the engagement
myself. I didn't go round to see the manager and
ask him how his poor thirst was, and then gently
insinuate as we lounged over the bar that I could
save him a lot of money if he would let me do an
extra turn. No ; I was a young, ambitious, un-
married artiste, with no influence to back me. My
parents were known in the profession as Mr. and
Mrs. Johnny Wilde, and they acted as my agents.
I went on with them in my ladies' stockings as an
acrobat. I didn't sing or patter, but mostly looked
at the audience, and wondered what they were

wasting their time there for, and I didn't get very good money for that.

On the second night there was an alarm of fire. My dad picked up a pair of opera glasses and looked round the stage to find me (I was so small that I used to get mislaid or slip in a chink between the boards), and then he picked me up with his finger and thumb.

I remember quite distinctly there was an artiste engaged there who showed some performing goats. He was a fat German, but he climbed on the roof in the general confusion with wonderful agility, and as soon as he reached there he screamed out, "Mein Gott! Mein Gott! Push me up mein goats; push dem up!" I don't know what sort of performance his goats would have given on the roof; but, fortunately, somebody threw a bucket of water over him and he seemed to recover.

This reminds me of a friend of mine who, with only the assistance of his wife, tried to carry a small billiard table down a long flight of stairs.

It was a good start, and they got to the bottom in the following order after a rattling finish :

        (1) My friend.

        (2) His wife.

        (3) Billiard table.

Won by a neck ; very bad third indeed.

The first performance I have been telling you about took place at the Cosmo Theatre Hall, Bell Street, Paddington.

And talking about bells, in Belfast I remember that a man of sin was very anxious to go to heaven, and his dodge was this—it may be useful for some of you. He presented a bell to a little chapel in a very religious neighbourhood, and when he died he left £50 to a man to ring this bell every morning and remind the good people to pray for him to go to heaven. Well, they knew what sort of a man he was and they didn't want to meet him in heaven, so they weren't going to pray, not they.

But—that was before they heard the bell. It started at eight o'clock in the morning the day after he died, and in three minutes the whole neighbourhood was in an uproar. It sounded just like throwing big stones at a cracked bucket, only many times magnified.

Well, they sent a deputation to the bell-puncher.

"Look here, we can't stand this," they said. The man didn't hear them at first, because he had to have his ears stuffed with lamb's wool to save his life. When he took the plugs out he told them that as soon as the man of sin entered heaven the bell would stop, and so they'd better go and pray for him as hard as they could.

"But if you like," he said, "I don't like this job, it's too dangerous for my taste, you can pay me to leave off. I've got £50 left me, but I lose it if I stop ringing. Now then, P.P., pray or pay, that's a fair bargain!"

Well, they thought they had better try praying

first, and they took a half-holiday for it, but next morning the bell was worse than ever.

"The old bounder must have taken the wrong turning," they said; "we'd better give the bell-ringer £60 and settle it."

So they soon got the money subscribed, because they felt some satisfaction in knowing they would keep the man of sin out of heaven. They had a list drawn up, headed like this :—

List of subscriptions for preserving heaven as an open space for the use of regular church-goers, and for the relief of residuary bell-ringers.

His Worship the Mayor £5   5   0
             &c.   *&c.*

Well, they took the money round and got a receipt for it, and then, as there was about £5 over, they had an impromptu tea-meeting for general rejoicings, and went home to bed feeling very pleased with themselves.

And the next morning—would you believe it?—the bell was going again just the same, only more so.

Off they rushed to the chapel, taking the receipt with them, to demand an explanation. What was their astonishment when they found another man there pulling at the rope.

"What's the meaning of this?" they yelled.

The man said, "Are you the subscribers?"

"Yes, we are. Why is not this nuisance stopped?"

"Well, ye see, it's this way," said the man; "the ould gint left £50 for the dam row, but he didn't care who was to do it, particular. Jim Blakey got the job first, and when you bought him off—I'm his brother—he give it me."

But that's an indigression. Let me on with my autobiography.

When I was five years of age I had an accident, and I decided to give up the profession of acrobacy and start as a dancer. My brother taught me a few steps, and we travelled as the Brothers Leno. My mother had married again, and my step-father made me a wedding present of the name of Leno.

The Brothers Leno made their first appearance at a North London music-hall, on a stage which was surrounded with mirrors. When we had finished we were so excited that we turned round to make our exit, rushed bang against the glass, flattened our noses, and concussed with such force that we both recoiled violently and sat down, feeling as if the hall was going round.

But the audience thought it was part of the show, and applauded so loudly that we had to go on and do it again; only after that rehearsal we took care not to damage ourselves so much. It just shows how devoted I was to my profession at that tender age that when my brother asked if I was hurt, I said, "Yes, I am; but didn't they like it!"

It's wonderful how things strike you sometimes,

especially when they're well aimed. For instance, look at eggs; you can't say an egg is neither here nor there, because it is. As a rule it is all over you, whether it's the new-laid egg, now almost extinct, or the fresh egg, or the egg, or the cooking egg.

A pot. Dog on the mantlepiece in my lodgings.

When you are applauded with eggs you must come under the yolk. However, that's a painful subject, and I will not pursue it *ab ovo* into *medias res*.

In 1869 my parents went to Glasgow to fulfil a fortnight's engagement, and it was there I met an ambitious boy called Jack, who has been my fast chum ever since. He was very fond of demons, I remember, and when I used to go for

c

a walk with the little girl that lived on the next floor at our lodgings he would walk behind us rubbing his hands fiendishly, and putting his finger against his nose, making believe he was Mephistopheles and we were Faust and Marguerite, until he was at last so demonish as to tie a cracker to little Marguerite's frock, and then we always made Mephistopheles walk in front where we could see what he was up to.

Talking about Mephistopheles reminds me of two plumbers with whom I had a most desperate encounter once. It's such a blood-curdling, melo-dramatic sketch that I must do it justice in a separate chapter.

CHAPTER   *Comedian* versus

THIRD   *Two Plumbers*

THE bath was of no use to me, and as it was
in a roomy room I thought I would have it
shifted (the bath, not the room), and make it into
a nursery for the children (the room, not the bath).

Accordingly, I pulled myself together one morning, and took a deep breath and walked into a
plumber's shop to implore his assistance, and
about nine o'clock the next morning he sent me
two pantomimists, who could have earned nearly
as much money at the halls as they did by
plumbing. One was a very tall man with whiskers
growing over his face like creepers, and just cut
off to leave room for his eyes, like windows. The
other was a small men's size and he had no
whiskers, but he had put on an apron that was
about as big as a tablecloth, suitable for a picnic
for thirty squatters.

It was crinkled up round his neck like the old-
fashioned ruff that Queen Elizabeth had to take off
before Shakespeare could kiss her when he went
courting, then it was folded half a dozen times
round his waist—well, the place where his waist

was before it got mislaid : it was only an imaginary line, like the equator really ; and then it fell in accordion pleats to the ground, and he hitched it up when he walked, like a girl crossing a muddy road.

Well, to go on with the story, they began their work of destruction as soon as they entered the house. The long tubular man butted the hall lamp like a wild goat on stilts and smashed it to powder, and the little globular man trod on his apron three times going upstairs, fell on his face and stained the carpet with his bleeding nose—all on purpose, I know, because it was a dirty apron, and he must have had a lot of practice in managing it. I asked him why he didn't carry a bit of gas piping in each hand and wave his apron about like a serpentine dancer, and he said, with a studious air, that he never thought of that.

When they reached the bath-room they sat down and looked at the bath as if they had never seen one before, and as if they were waiting to see it perform.

Then the short one got up and stroked and patted it with his hand, as if he was telling it to be a good bath.

" Oh ! " I said, " don't be afraid ; it isn't savage."

He turned round and murmured something to his colleague, and sat down again with a sigh. They had some more low conversation and lit their pipes, and I was just wondering whether I ought to offer to fill the bath with beer and get them to carry it

that way when the other one got up and rapped
with his knuckles on it, and then scratched his
whiskers, put both hands in his trousers pockets,
and grunted.

Then, having shown that they were not afraid
of it, they turned their attention to the pictures
on the walls, and had an argument about their
respective merits. Without coming to any unani-
mous decision they went away, saying that they
were going to fetch their tools and would be back
in half an hour.

They returned five hours later with enough tools
to build a row of houses with, and as the procession went upstairs again they let a hammer fly
out of one of the baskets, which nearly brained me
as I came behind them. They laughed genially,
while I rubbed my head. When we got into the
room they put down the baskets and resumed their
art criticisms. It appears that one had declared the
figures in a picture to be angels, while the other
was confident that they were ostriches, and now,
on taking a second look, the man that had backed
the angels admitted that he was wrong, although
he had had a run for his money, he said, and he
paid over to the ostrich - fancier. Would you
believe it ?—the picture in dispute was a little
pathetic effort of my own, entitled " Heavenwards."

After that they came back from art to science,
and slowly emptied their baskets of all sorts of
fearful and wonderful implements and materials,

which were strewn all over the floor. There was
a long piece of wire, the use of which I did not
understand until I saw Whiskers cleaning his pipe
with it. And Apron showed me a lantern, which,
by some pumping arrangement, shot out a large
flame about a foot long, and enabled Whiskers
to get his pipe well alight without striking a lot
of matches.

Apron was very pleased with his lantern,
and kept pumping it with an expression on his
face that might have indicated that he had
conquered Europe. At last he put it on the
floor with the flame flaring away, and went to
his basket to find a lead pencil. He brought
this back to sharpen with a hatchet, and while
he was doing this set his apron on fire with the
lantern. Whiskers made a heroic rescue of him.
Seizing the apron he swung the globular man
round the room, but burnt his fingers, and suddenly dropped his colleague, who fell on the back
of his head, and stayed there for a few moments'
rest and quiet.

The long man went back to his work. He had
ceased to be a knockabout, and had become a
musical clown, and he was hitting the bath with
a hammer to try and make it sing "The Village
Blacksmith."

Meanwhile Apron put some lead in a spoon,
and proceeded to melt it by means of the lantern.
I thought perhaps he was going to put a plug
in the back of his head where he fell, because

I could not see any other possible use for melted lead in that scene. When it was nicely simmering he put the spoon on the floor, and took the lantern into a corner where it would be away from the sweep of the train of his apron. The tall man tried to reach a chisel with his right hand without relinquishing his hold on the bath, and losing his balance he kicked the molten lead all over the oilcloth, setting it on fire in several spots. They both laughed and apologised, and said accidents would happen.

Then they threw a pail of water over the burning oilcloth, and the water flowed under the door and downstairs, and when I looked on the landing I saw the baby sitting in it, crying. I picked the damp baby up and took it to a place of safety, as far from the plumbers as possible, and when I came back, I found, to my great satisfaction, that the tall man had smashed his thumb with the musical hammer, and the little man had fallen off a pair of steps into the bath.

I asked them as calmly as I could whether they had come there to commit suicide or to burn me out of house and home, and they looked displeased. To console themselves they sat down and had some bread and cheese and beer, and as they didn't invite me to join them I went away for an hour, after which I returned and found them both fast asleep.

"Well," I said to myself, "I think too much of this is enough," so I woke Whiskers with a pin

and Apron with the lantern, and they sat up and
started a long conversation about some dogs,
which lasted until it was time for them to go
home, when they got up as if they had earned
a good rest and asked me for some beer money,
promising to come early next morning.

I ought to mention that they took the bath
with them and only let it fall downstairs twice,
breaking the umbrella - stand in the hall and
making an infernal noise. They say if you put
a number of tin çans and a table at the top of
a flight of steps and push them down all together
you get the general effect of a Chinese orchestra;
but this bath and umbrella-stand duet sounded
like massed bands playing the Chinese army
quadrilles.

Now it—and here comes the most thrilling part
of my tale—it happened that in the ceiling over
the bath there was a large "rose" for a cold
shower, which could be turned on by pulling a
chain. Well, these clever men took the chain
away and left the tap turned on, or made some
mistake of the kind. I was sleeping in the room
underneath the bath-room, and early next morning I was roused by drops of water falling on the
bed, and looking up I saw that the ceiling was
completely saturated. I rushed upstairs in my
pyjamas and found a beautiful waterfall coming
from the shower-bath arrangement. What was
to be done? If it ran much longer I should have
the whole family afloat in tubs and wash-bowls.

I got a bucket and put it under the shower, and when that was full I put down another and hurried downstairs to empty the first. Before I could get back the second one was running over, and I played this game until nine o'clock, when the pantomimists returned.

How they laughed! Why, the tears coursed down their cheeks as they sat on the stairs enjoying the fun.

I said, "There's water enough in the house already. What is there to laugh at?"

Then they told me how it had all come about. It seems that they had forgotten to lift the cistern ball or something of that kind—I was too mad to listen to them.

Since then I have become an enthusiastic anti-plumbist. I have no objection to plumbers in the abstract, but I don't like them in my house.

CHAPTER	Baggage
FOURTH	*Adventures*

I FORGET where I was when I interrupted my autobiography to claim your sympathy in my plumbing troubles; but at that time of my life I was never long in one place.

My parents had gone to Edinburgh for a fortnight's engagement in 1867, and they intended to return to London at once; but it was not until 1881 that I reappeared in the metropolis, and in the meantime I had been all over England, Scotland, and Ireland. It was in Dublin that I was first discovered by the public as the possessor of a lovely voice, and as an Irish comic singer I was very successful, earning a high salary for my seven years. At Manchester we produced a spectacular ballet, called " The Wicklow Wedding," in which I played the principal part and painted the scenery.

A rather amusing incident occurred in connection with a Liverpool engagement. When we arrived, in order to maintain the dignity of our little company, I got some money from the manager to pay for our luggage being taken to the theatre

instead of taking it ourselves. I called a man
with a hand-cart, whose respectfulness touched
me deeply because he was a good deal better

DAN LENO

THE PROPRIETOR OF THE 19TH CENTURY STORES.

dressed than I was. He loaded his cart with
our curious assortment of baggage. There was
a trick bedstead which, bundled together and tied

round with rope, was not at all an object of
beauty suitable for a nobleman's furniture, and
an old tin tray tied in with string formed the
bottom of one of the baskets, so that when the
cart was piled up with the things it looked more
like a cheap eviction than the arrival of a troop of
respectable professionals.

We were to open at the Adelphi Theatre in
Christian Street, and we told the man to take the
things to the Adelphi. He touched his cap and
went, while I decided that, as I had plenty of
time, I would have a walk round the town before
going to the theatre, and still reach there as soon
as the porter; so away I went and bought some
cakes with twopence of the money that the
manager had given me to pay the man with.
I have a vivid recollection of these cakes, which
were of an extremely obstinate nature with a
speck of jam in the middle. I remember hammer-
ing one on a doorstep in order to chip a piece off,
and I gave the other to some little girls, who licked
off the jam and played hopscotch with the rest.

When I arrived at the theatre in about an hour's
time I found no porter and no luggage. I spread
myself all over the town to look for him, and you
can imagine my surprise when I discovered the
man with the bedstead on his back engaged in
violent altercation with two liveried servants on
the steps of the Adelphi Hotel in Lime Street.
He insisted on putting the luggage in, and the
hotel was in a state of siege. The basket, with

the tin-tray false bottom, had been pitched out
by the hotel people so energetically that it had
fallen to pieces, and the "props" were scattered
all over the muddy street. My porter was un-
daunted. He had been told to put the things in
the Adelphi, and he would have them in if it
killed him. It was a noble and sublime spectacle,
but our belongings were being seriously depreci-
ated. Some small boys amongst the interested
crowd had found a stuffed dog which had come out
of the basket, and they were playing football with
it, and when I went to rescue the poor, dumb,
stuffed creature they played football with me.

At last, with the dog under my arm and my
clothes covered with mud, I succeeded in getting
near enough to the porter to explain things. He
was disappointed. I shall never forget the look
on the man's face if I live to be ninety-nine. I
never saw a man look with such an earnest desire
to take a human life as he did, and had he raised
the bedstead and brained me where I stood I
should not have been at all surprised. I should
have been sorry, but not surprised.

Well, we collected the scattered property in the
face of a withering fire of criticism from the crowd,
and then the porter and I, with the cart, headed a
long procession marching to the theatre. Liverpool
mud is very muddy indeed, and I was not happy.
Even then our troubles were not ended, for when
we reached Christian Street one of the wheels
came off the confounded cart, and once again

our poor "props" were upset in the slimy road. For the fourteenth time our porter repeated his entire vocabulary of obscene and profane terms of general abuse and condemnation, and sent me into a cold perspiration at the fearful language he used.

And when at length I reached the theatre, tired, hungry, muddy, almost in tears, I held out my hand to reward the honest labourer for his toil. I gave him all the money I had left—*one shilling*. It was a thrilling situation. The man staggered; there was a wild glare in his eyes; his breath came and went in short snorts; he clenched his fists, and—like the heroes of romance—I knew no more.

Not long after I had more trouble with the same baggage. We were engaged to appear at the Britannia Music-hall, Sheffield, and of course arrived on the Monday. Father and mother went to look for our lodgings and left me to get the luggage to the hall, and prepare it for our performance in the evening. I went and borrowed a hand-cart—cabs were out of the question with us in those days, and after a good deal of exertion and deep thought, managed to take the things to the theatre, which I found in total darkness.

However, I put the baggage on the stage, except some costumes that I took upstairs to the dressing-room. We were playing a sketch called "Pongo the Monkey," in which we used our trick bedstead, and it was necessary to bore a hole in the stage in which to fix a strong wooden upright that formed the mainstay of the bed. I got the large auger we used for the purpose; but the hall was so dark that I couldn't see what I was doing, so I kept striking matches to look how I was going on. After I had finished boring I went away to fetch something, and when I returned I was horrified to see a light shining through the hole I had bored. I guessed at once that I must have dropped a match through the hole and set the stage on fire.

There was not a moment to be lost. Off I dashed to the dressing-room and seized a bucket of water. When I rushed back the light seemed brighter, and I did not waste a moment in pouring the water through the hole, and then waited with beating heart to see the result. Had the whole heatre burst into flames I should not have been so astonished as I was, for the result came in vocal form. A gruff voice under the stage exclaimed :

"What ta devil is ta doin' oop thear? Does ta want ter drownd me?" Then there was the sound of hurried and heavy footsteps.

I was always pretty nimble on my feet, but that time I think I beat all records. I shot out of the building before you could say James Brown.

From cautious and discreet enquiries I made afterwards I learned that underneath the stage was used by the proprietor as a stable for his pony, and the man who came to look after the animal had fortunately placed himself in the best possible position for receiving my bucketful. It couldn't have gone better if it had been rehearsed for a fortnight.

That reminds me of another little incident which has nothing whatever to do with it.

We were to appear at the old Britannia Music-hall, Coventry, a town I was always very fond

View of. a Colliery Village

of, and as soon as I had washed my breakfast and swallowed myself off I used to go into the country to make little water-colour sketches of any picturesque spots that attracted my critical eye.

But I want to work off a little anecdote I remember at the moment. There was a man

who used to give a turn with some performing
birds. Oh, it was a beautiful show! it used to
please the women especially—women have such
a lot of sentiment for exhibition purposes. There
were half a dozen peacocks that used to expand
and fold their splendid tails to the tune of a
waltz played by the orchestra. It was too lovely
for this world, it reminded one of heaven. But,
luckily, one evening the birds gave a sort of
extra turn on their own account; for the man's
assistant had forgotten to fasten their feet on the
stage, and when the band struck up they simply
strutted away. But they would have astonished
Bo-Peep as much as they astonished the audience; for instead of bringing their tails behind
them they left them there: the birds had no tails
of their own at all. Still, as the waltz played the
show went on all the same, the tails spread out
and closed up again, until the curtain came down
suddenly, amidst tremendous applause. It was
done by a boy pulling a string at the side of
the stage.

That's a digression. Where was I? Oh,
Coventry! Well, they tell you a story at
Coventry which, perhaps, you haven't heard.
It's about a certain Mrs. Godiva, and I'll tell it
you just as it was told me.

D

CHAPTER   *That Coventry*
FIFTH   *Story*

THE man that told me this incredible story
was supposed to be a respectable, married,
level-headed, flat-footed, natural-born man with
no particular crimes on his conscience beyond
doing his fellow-men, as often as the law would
let him, just the same as you would yourself.
He was quite ordinary to look at, except that
he had a bunion on the back of his neck, and
they had to cut a sort of pigeon-hole, as it were,
in his collar, to give the bunion free play. He
was about two sizes bigger than me, and so I had
to listen to his story right through, although when
he came to the most horrible part of it I was so
disgusted that once I raised a jug to throw at
him, only he happened to turn round and reveal
his bunion, and I felt so full of pity for him that
I contented myself with dropping the jug on his
toes. I have a soft-roed heart.

Well, this is the story; get your blushes ready.
I assure you, in the course of a long and stormy
and red and blue career, I never heard anything
like it.

This is how the man started.

I must tell you that he had a shocking cold in his head, and could not pronounce his words distinctly.

"A good beddy years ago," he said, "it appears dere was a certaid barod or brewer or some sort of a swell joker who was boss of Covedry—the whole bloomig place. Ad it happed one year dere was a kide of rebelliod. They woulded pay dere gas bill or water rate or somethig. Ad this barod whed he went roud to collect the modey was insulted ad tode to go to blazes or Birmighab, which wasset codvediet at that tibe. So he ups and he says, 'We'll dab well see about dis.' Of course they diddet speak exactly the sabe lagguage ded, but that was the effect of his words. Ad he wedt ad turd the water off and surrouded the place with his vassals."

"I beg pardon," I interrupted, "did you say his gassals?"

"Doh, vassals, sort of Hooligad gag that he was captaid of. Ad he was goig to wipe the floor with the whole populatiod. Well, here cobes his wife Godiva. She cobes ad sits od his dee."

"On his what?" I cried.

"Od his dee."

"Oh, yes, I see. But it must have been hundreds of years ago for a wife to sit on her husband's knee. Now, if it had been anybody else's——"

"Gospel truth, she did. Why, she was so

affectiodate that his trousers used to get warred out every two or three years, and she had to put patches od. Well, to cut a log trouser—I mead story—short, he probised to let theb off——"

"What, the trou——"

"Doh, the people."

"Oh, of course. Gave me quite a shock."

"Od wod conditiod. Ad wat d'you thig that was?"

"What the condition was? I dunno. That they'd tip him the winner of next year's Derby?"

"Doh."

"Well, then, they'd give him and his ancestors free drinks at all the local bars except on bank holidays?"

"Doh, dothig of that kide; you're looking at it frob a personal poid of view. Doh, the codditiod was"—here the bunion bearer dropped his voice, leaned towards me and breathed a quantity of four-ale fumes down my ear—"that his wife, Godiva, should ride daked through the streets of Covedry."

Well, I tell you I blushed from the crown of my head to the roots of my hair when I heard that. You could have knocked me down with a crowbar.

"Ride nake——" I gasped.

"Id a state," said the man, "id a state of dudity."

"But," I said, thinking I'd settled him, "bicycles weren't invented then, so how could she?"

"She diddet ride od a bicycle; od a horse!"

"Oh, a bareback act!" I said.

"Very," replied the man.

'And do you mean to tell me that the 'buses were running all the time?" I protested.

Then he went on to tell me that everybody stayed indoors and wouldn't look at this Mrs. Godiva, except a man called Peeping Tom, with whom I have no doubt you have a certain amount of sympathy. Now there are about a hundred houses in Coventry, every one of which claims to have the window from which Thomas peeped, so that I think it's all Peeping Tommy rot, or else there were a great many people of that name. If he was the only person that saw the lady, who was it that brought the horse out and helped her on? Moreover, besides, was it a blind horse? I think the whole story is blind myself. I can't imagine a lot of people acting like that. Do you think any married woman of the present day— I don't care how high she might be in society— would consent to ride naked through a town if she knew beforehand that nobody was going to look at her? Why, it's simply preposterous!

CHAPTER SIXTH   *A Melodramatic Sketch*

A T that time of life I used to feel sometimes as if I was walking on air instead of the ground, perhaps because I had not sufficient ballast inside to keep me from soaring heavenwards. I used to laugh and sing for no other reason than that I couldn't help it; whereas now I want somebody to make me laugh.

It was on a lovely morning once that I set out from Coventry to walk to Kenilworth. I took with me my colour boxes (price 9*d*.), portfolio (two pieces of cardboard with a strip of canvas glued on one side, and two pieces of tape tied together on the other side, price 2*d*., and a little labour), and water bottle. I had been walking along Warwick Road about an hour when I was greatly struck with the appearance of the loveliest old house I had ever seen, and the picture it presented in the morning sun, as it stood there— well, of course, you wouldn't expect it to skip about, I know—surrounded by stately old trees with their rich autumn tints, was more than I could withstand.

Daddie Thicumbe Pantomime
Drury Lane 1891
Yours truly
Dan Leno

So I said to myself, " I 'm going to climb the fence and sketch that house. It's never done anything to me, but I 'll sketch it all the same." There was a board up—a picturesque board— telling me that trespassers would be prosecuted; but I didn't think they would take the trouble to prosecute me. Over I went, and when I decided which was the best view of the house, I squatted down and started sketching.

However, before I had done much harm my blood curdled in my veins at the sound of a deep, hollow, come-up-for-judgment-when-called-upon sort of voice.

"What are you doing here?" said the owner of the voice; and the portfolio fell from my trembling hand. Looking round I beheld a tall, gaunt, cadaverous old gentleman, dressed all in black, looking at me with a pair of very small, cruel eyes. I really thought at first he had come up through a trap from the infernal regions.

I pulled myself together, nevertheless.

"I beg pardon, sir," I said, "but I was so charmed with the beauty of your house that I ventured to stop and make a sketch of it." My presence of mind was all the more commendable, seeing that, in my first surprise, I had put the water bottle in my pocket upside down with the cork out, and I was not feeling at all comfortable during my speech.

"And when," said the gloomy stranger, "do you think the sketch will be finished?"

"In ten minutes, sir."

"Very well, don't go away. I should like to see it. I'll return in ten minutes' time."

With that he disappeared. I don't know where he went; he simply dissolved into the air.

The moment he vanished I grabbed all my belongings, and made a mad bull rush at the fence.

But suddenly I stopped and recovered from my panic. "Oh, there's nothing to be afraid of," I said, "I'll finish the picture. He may give me something for it. And if he's the devil," and I really thought he might be, "well, what's the good of running away?"

Down I sat and hurried to finish the sketch, and just as I put the last touch to it that ghostly figure was there again, standing at my elbow.

I nearly swallowed the brush which I had put between my teeth to hold.

"Is the picture done?" said the fiend, in his tombstone voice.

"Yes, sir." He took it in his long, bony hands.

"What are you going to do with it?"

"Oh, I shall keep it as a pleasant memento ——"

"You will do nothing of the kind," shrieked the old gentleman, growing excited, "I want it myself—I want it myself—Ha, ha! a picture of the house! Ha, ha, ha, ha, ha!"

His laughter was positively demoniacal, and I felt that my last hour had come as he danced

round me, pointing at me with his skinny fore-
finger. Then he seized my hand and shouted
"Begone! Begone!". and disappeared again.

Instead of begoing I felt as if I had taken root
there. In my hand was half a sovereign, which
I expected every second to see burst into flames.
But gradually my circulation improved, and leaving
colour boxes, water bottle, and everything else on
the ground I made a second wild charge at the
fence. Whether I jumped over it, wriggled under
it, broke through it, or pushed it down I know
not, but I know that I never stopped running till
I was quite a mile away from the place.

I afterwards learned that the poor old gentleman was a lunatic, and that I had been sketching
the side of the house where his wife committed
suicide by jumping through a window.

CHAPTER
SEVENTH
*A Skating
Romance*

WHEN I was early in my teens I thought it
as well to add roller-skating to my accom-
plishments, and I studied with enthusiasm. It is
wonderful what man can do on his first pair of
skates. Things seem to him to wear a different
aspect altogether; the ground acts in a most
mysterious way: sometimes it is hovering over
your head and sometimes waltzing round you.
But there is one sure thing—you can always find
it : you have only to follow your nose, and there
it is.

It was when I was fulfilling an engagement not
far from the pretty little village of Birmingham
that I was vaccinated with skates for the first
time. There was a large rink adjoining the hall,
and I went with a very benevolent man, who
showed me the whole art. He said I was to rise
from my seat and strike out. I did so, and landed
nicely on his upper lip.

Then he took me by the hand and we slid off
together. I really do not know what happened.
Clouds seemed to be flying round me; houses and
concert halls were in the air, darting about like

swallows; trees were dancing upside down, and my kind friend was bobbing about in various fantastic forms. I wriggled and curled and twisted and crouched and kicked, but I did not feel at all comfortable until I suddenly found myself sitting on the good man's face.

Well, I suggested after that that I should try it with my arm round his neck; but he said he would like to see his home once more, so I did not insist. After struggling for a quarter of an hour I managed to get up on my feet again, and plunged wildly into a corner. I seemed to be dashing to destruction at about two hundred miles an hour; but with great presence of mind I got a firm grip of a man's hair. I plucked a handful from him, which was sufficient to attract his attention. He kicked me twice with great energy, and then punched me behind so forcibly that I butted into the chest of a tall man with indignant whiskers, who, after my charge, seemed to whiz round like a catherine wheel. When he finally collapsed I was lying across his neck, and a small boy was underneath both of us. I left them to unravel themselves, and hobbled off on my hands and knees to find my friend. He had bound a handkerchief round his battered head, and his swollen nose looked like a boiled carrot. He was apologizing to a lady for having passionately embraced her to save his life, and while he was bowing his excuses down he went on his face again.

When I reached home my people thought I had been struck by lightning, and I was so sore all over that it was very painful work dancing that night. However, I went back the next morning, and I soon advanced in the art.

Now it happened that there was a refreshment bar in the place. You know what a refreshment bar is, I suppose? Yes; I thought you did. Well, and there was a very refreshing barmaid there as well. A barmaid, I ought to explain, is—— Oh, you know, do you? Wonderful thing this spread of education!

And at that tender age I thought she was an angel that had come down from heaven to draw corks for thirsty men and flavour the beer with her smiles. I have always been a champion of women; I always defend their cause. I maintain that they are the best wives and mothers and sisters on earth. All men are kickers, except me. Man blames woman for every accident and misfortune under the sun, moon, stars, table, or bed. He sneers at her curiosity. Why, he is far more curious himself. I know, because I have made experiments.

Some time since I put up a board outside my door with the words "Wet Paint" on it. In less than an hour I counted more than forty men that came and clapped their hands or their thumbs on the door to see if the paint really was wet. Some of them seemed disgusted, and others showed a childish pleasure in their cleverness.

One man was so persevering—he wanted to give the door every chance—that he leaned against it for ten minutes, and then went away with a terrible look of disappointment to call on his solicitor, and see if he couldn't sue me for damages.

But look at the sweeter sex. Paint does not interest them. There was not one of the many women who read that warning that touched it with her glove, or her bonnet, or even brushed her skirt against it. The awful temptation was there, but they overcame it. And they gathered their frocks up and trotted away on their toes to escape the danger.

What is that atom of barloafing clay called man? What is he good for? He does not know the magnitude of woman's operations. He does not know—till I tell him—that the women of England—the noble, devoted creatures—in one year lost 595,000,000 hairpins. What can he do to compare with that? Woman can come to a final conclusion without the slightest trouble of reasoning, and that is a thing no sane man can do. She can keep as cool as a cucumber in a tight-fitting dress, and dance all night in a pair of shoes two sizes less than her foot, and smile all the time. She can drive a man crockery-smashing crazy for twenty-four hours, and then raise him to paradise by simply tickling his chin. Where is the man that can do that? I do not believe in the superiority of man, and I expect

that in years to come woman will make herself more and more felt—with anything that's handy.

To resume my romance. At that time I fell heavily in love with this beautiful barmaïd, and I used to do all my graceful turns up at her end of the room in order to smite her.

I remember that my costume consisted of a pair of trousers that I had long grown out of, a waistcoat that did not reach so far as to meet them half way, and a sort of zouave jacket, while on my head was a faithful old Scotch cap. So that you will see that I did not depend on fine clothes for making an impression, only on my natural, unadorned loveliness.

But one day I was presented with a new pair of trousers, which cost 3*s*. 11*d*., and were of a haunting beauty. They were very light and gay in colour, with a vocal check pattern —three checks on one leg and two on the other; and I set out for the rink full of renewed hope. It was raining hard and I got very wet, but I cared not; and as soon as I reached the rink away I glided up to the bar and began my manœuvres.

But I was surprised to see that the girl kept turning her head away with her handkerchief to her mouth, and all the people near me were grinning and pointing. I didn't know what to make of it—until I felt rather cool around the ankles, and then I looked down and saw that there were only two checks on the leg that had three before, and the damp trousers were visibly crawling up my legs. They modestly shrunk from publicity.

Of course I scampered home as fast as I could, and just got inside the door as the trousers were hurrying over my knees; but I never recovered my lost reputation. Love will not survive ridicule, and the lover ought to make sure that he is fast colour and thoroughly shrunk before he starts out. I have always taken care since.

E

CHAPTER EIGHTH

Barbers I have Met

IN the course of a rolling career I have managed to grow a little moss on the lower half of my face, and every few weeks I have to have it sawn off by a hairdresser's labourer. When I am in London this is not a painful process in itself, and I consider it valuable moral training to carry on a cheerful conversation with a lathery brush frisking round your mouth, especially in the winter when the young man caresses your jaw with his cold fingers. Personally I never try to say much. I always mumble the word "yes," until the young shaver comes to the catechism about shampoo and singeing and hair restoring, and then I say "no" in my most pathetic voice. We go on like this:

"Cold day, sir."

"Yes."

"Think it's going to rain if it doesn't keep dry?"

"Yes."

"Seen that case, sir, of the man that's charged with assaulting his wife by giving her her housekeeping money twice over last week?"

"Yes."

"Think he did it on purpose, or kind of absent-minded?"

"Yes."

"Shampoo, sir?"

"Ye—no."

"Like your hair watered, sir? Been very dry weather lately."

"No."

"Have some of our spirituous hair-raiser, sir? Wonderful stuff. Grow you a moustache like two horses' tails."

"No."

"Thank you, sir. Pay at the desk, please."

That is the ordinary sort of dialogue; but in the country you meet some very curious whisker choppers.

I went once to a little shop in the Midlands to have my golden flax mowed off, and the labourer there was really stupid. He came and asked me if I wanted a shave, and I said "yes," and then he went clean away and sat down in a corner with his head resting in his hands, as if he was buried in deep thought, or as if he had never shaved a man before and was studying how he could safely begin. He had no apron or anything of that sort on.

When he returned I leaned back with my chin in the air, and he put his hand under it and looked down on me with such a sad and compassionate expression that I sat up again and looked round at the door. But he smiled en-

couragingly, as if to assure me that it would soon
be over, and so I dropped my head back on the
rest again, and tried to sit on my shoulder blades.

Still he did not start. He felt the blades of
two or three razors with his thumb, and then he
said—

"Now, sir, how would you like to be shaved—
by the square inch, or by the piece?"

I sat up again more suddenly than before.
"What the——"

"Oh! it's our new system in this town," he
said; "if you want your beard slitting here, I'll
just measure it and give you an estimate. It's
five inches for a penny. But if you'll have it
done by the piece I'll make a good job of it for
threepence-halfpenny."

"Oh, well," I said, "that's a bit steep, but go
ahead and look alive."

"Look alive, sir? Yes, sir." And he bounced
into the middle of the room and started vigorous
stage dancing.

"Stop that!" I yelled.

"Told me to look alive, didn't you, sir? I did
my best. Well, then," he continued genially, "let's
to business."

He took up the biggest hairbrush in the shop,
smothered it in lather, and turned round to hit me
on the jaw with it.

But I wasn't there. I had crawled under the
chair for safety.

What further would have happened I don't

know, but just then another barber came in with his apron on. He went straight up to my shaver and handed him his wages, and the man put on his hat and walked out.

"What d' you have a man like that in your shop for?" I grumbled.

"Oh, that's an actor, sir, playing at the Royal this week—Mr. Fred Leslie, sir. I had to pop out and get change for him."

An interesting specimen of the small provincial hairdresser's labourer came up to me once with a shaving brush in his hand, and asked me if I wanted my hair cutting. This was only a dodge of his to get me to open my mouth, and as soon as I started to reply he dabbed the brush in and began lathering my face all over. Then he put his left arm round my neck firmly and with a rough right hand like emery paper began massaging my soapy face until I writhed in my seat. I couldn't shout because he had gagged me with soap, and I couldn't open my eyes for it either. At last he released me and began stropping his razor, smiling at me with great satisfaction.

"Pleasant morning, sir," he remarked.

"B-r-r-r-h," I spluttered, "it's the pleasantest morning I've known since I fell into the river."

The master barber saw that I was not happy, and he came to relieve his assistant. As he began to scrape my poor grated chin he told me that the young man had only just come to the shop, and had not been there long.

Now that was a piece of information to ponder over. I kept turning it over in my mind until it gave me a severe headache. You see, of course, if he had only just come he could not possibly have been there long. On the other hand, if he had been there long he could not have only just come.

Then again, here is another serious aspect. If he had come long ago he would have been there a considerable time. Put it in another way. If the young man had already been there long before he had only just come, then it seems to follow that he must have come long before he had just been there. Let us work this thing out properly. If this young man——

But at that moment I was roused from my reverie by the barber toying with a shred of skin he thought I did not want; and to cheer me up he put some scorching stuff on the cut that brought the long-pent-up tears into my eyes.

He passed his fingers through my hair and asked me if I would take a bottle of his Klondike Lime Spruce.

"Is it good?" I asked nonchalantly.

"Best in the trade, sir; never fails."

"Well, then, that man at Brighton was a fabricator of untruthfulnesses!" I exclaimed. "He said that the very best thing was his Californian Gum Gum Cream. Now who is speaking the truth?"

"Well, sir," he said, "you just try it, and if you

become bald after using Klondike Lime Spruce
I'll give you a free season ticket that will entitle
you to have your hair cut for nothing, there! I
wouldn't make an offer like that if I wasn't
confident, would I?"

"It's a small bottle for three shillings."

"It is small, sir; but you only require three drops."

"Well, I'd better have four drops, I might
spill one."

"I can't break a bottle, sir."

"Not necessary to break it," I observed; "take
the cork out."

"Couldn't open a bottle either," he said.

"Well, how are you going to get the stuff out if
you can't open the bottle?"

"I don't think we understand each other," said
the barber with a troubled look. "What I meant
was that we couldn't open the bottle because it's
against our rule to break bottles."

"They must be funny bottles if you can't open
them without breaking them. Why don't you
bore a hole in them with a gimlet?"

"Like a shampoo, sir?" asked the barber in
a tired voice.

"Why don't you put the bottle in a hot oven
and make it sweat, so you can get the stuff out
and use the bottle again?"

"Hard or soft brush, sir?"

"Why don't you turn the bottle upside down
and then run away and pretend you're not looking
at it, and then it'll simply pour out?"

"Anything else you'd like, sir?'

"Well, some day I'd like to have a long talk about these bottles when you're not so busy. It seems to me a most interesting problem. Let's go into these bottles thoroughly. You say you can't open a bottle to break it, and of course it does seem unnecessary. And you can't break a bottle by opening it. Well, there may be some force in that. But look here, now. Supposing——"

"Thank you, sir; good-morning."

It's a mysterious profession, barberism. A hairdresser is not like other men. He is a man all by himself; he eats and drinks sometimes, but there is a something about him. He is a bay rum chap, the barber. He has a lather of conversation, but there is nothing in it that would razor brush—I mean, raise a blush—to the cheek of the most eccentric comedian on the music-hall stage.

CHAPTER NINTH

I go Pearl Fishing

I SEEM to have dropped my autobiography somewhere and gone rambling on these philosophical excursions; but the fact is that I am determined there shall be nothing but the truth in this literary work of mine. I have forgotten more about my early life than I ever knew, and I am not going to invent a lot of anecdotes and thrilling escapes from fire and water and brokers' men. No; I might romance, but I will not do anything of the kind. I go on telling the truth in my simple straightforward way if it kills me.

I was about seventeen when I was seized with a restless desire to roll on the ocean waves. I was in Liverpool at the time, and a friend persuaded me to set out with him for the pearl fisheries situated between Margate and Japan.

When we had got about as far as New Brighton after a fair passage, with the wind north-north by south-south, latitude nineteen and six, longitude three feet four, sea calm, but dirty, owing to it being the bathing season, a tempest arose.

My friend came rushing down from the roof into

the back parlour and said, "I say, old man, there's a terrific storm going on." He need not have taken the trouble. I knew it. In fact, I could have told him that, only just then the ship gave a violent heave as if it wasn't comfortable in its seat and I pitched head first into his chest, and we both went rolling on the floor, under a shower of tin cans and bottles from the shelves.

My friend got up and tried to look as if he had being doing this all his life, and as if he had been born on his beam ends, shivering his timbers.

He opened a bottle of ale and asked me what I would have. I thanked him kindly and said I would like a bucket, which he got me, and lashed me to it in case I should fall overboard and miss it.

He emptied his bottle of ale and I filled my bucket, which kept us amused, and passed the time away for a little while, until he asked me if I knew where we were going, and I answered that I knew of one or two sultry places where I should like him to go, and where I fancied I was going if this sort of thing went on much longer. He said, "Cheer up, we shall soon be there." And I told him I was there now, or as near as possible. Then he said—

"Never mind, only just a little more rough weather and I'll show you something you've never seen before."

"I wish I'd never seen this," I groaned. "If you've got any more novelties, you'd better keep them for the Christmas pantomime."

But he assured me that the captain had ordered the main jibboom to be spanked on the figure-head, so as to make all taut, and I felt much relieved to hear of this. .

Now I come to the most exciting part of the voyage.

The captain was a reckless, dare-devil sort of navvy, and he had decided to take a short cut across the Bospherranean, knowing all the time the fearful risk he was running of going too close to the Magnetic Islands. The drawing powers of these islands are so strong that they have the "House Full" boards out every day. No steel or iron can pass within three streets of it. We could see far off through our opera-glasses that there were half a dozen ironclads sticking to the rocks, deserted by their crews. But our careless captain only laughed and said his ship was all wood, and we were quite safe.

But we had got only half-way past the islands, and seemed to be gliding along smoothly, when suddenly we were very much surprised to see our paddle-wheels suddenly fly off the ship and go straight to land. We were simply thunderstruck. Then the funnel flew out and stuck to some trees; then away went the anchor. Next the buttons off the sailors' clothes shot off and fell like a shower of hail on the rocks, and there they stuck glittering in the sunlight. It was a pretty sight, but still, buttons are buttons—I won't labour the point.

Well, we thought we had got over the worst when up comes the engine, and off it goes through the air with the first mate hanging on to a crank. Poor first mate! He didn't want to go then at all. But, you see, he was wearing a steel watch-chain at the time, so he had to.

Then there was poor old Ben Bowsprit the Bosun. He was wearing a pair of hob-nailed boots at the time, and the magnetism dragged him off the ship feet foremost. When he reached the island he stuck to the same rocks by his feet, and was hanging head downwards until he could unlace his boots, drop into the sea and swim back to the ship.

The ultimate disaster was all owing to Ben's fatal passion for wearing these hobnailed boots. For when he reached the ship again it happened that all the nails had naturally been drawn out of the vessel by the islands, and when Ben took hold of the ship to pull himself on board it came to pieces in his hand, and we all found ourselves struggling in the ocean. I always blamed Ben for that.

Every one of us was drowned except myself, and I was saved by floating to the islands on the drawing-room door. You see the boats were good for nothing without any nails, and I just happened to get hold of this bit of solid timber. Of course I did my best for the crew. I pulled out my note-book and took down their last farewells in a sort of shorthand, and there wasn't one that I didn't say a kind word to. But I had in my hand a rolling-pin out of the kitchen, and when any of the poor fellows caught hold of my raft I had the presence of mind to hit them till they let go. You see, I had to be saved, because I was engaged to appear at a Liverpool hall, and I try never to disappoint the public.

Well, when I reached the land I was not out of my troubles, for there seemed to be nothing substantial to eat. There was no soup or fish or *entrées*, or any of those things; it was simply a desert island, and I was very hungry after my exercise. However, I seized my rolling-pin and stalked some mussels on the rocks. They are very stupid creatures, and you have only to knock them over with a stick; but you get tired of them for breakfast, dinner, and tea. I tried them raw, boiled, grilled, poached, scrambled, devilled, and *à la reine*.

Now the next thing I knew from my reading was to start keeping an almanac and building a hut. For the almanac I didn't worry, because I knew that I should get one of Aunt Beagle's Soothing Mixture's little books delivered to me as usual, and for building the house I went back to the ship, on my drawing-room door, and found a lot of empty sardine tins and tomato cans floating about, which I tied together and towed to shore.

With these and the mussel shells I soon erected a nice little seven-roomed, semi-detached villa, with a garden back and front, only three minutes from the nearest station and every modern convenience, and I called it "The Shells." Then I thought I had better not be idle in the place, so I stuck an imitation brass plate on the gate: "D. Leno, O.U.R.A., Professor of the Pianoforte and Phrenology; Painless Extractions."

I ought to tell you that the island I was on was only about six feet long by three and a quarter wide, and for my necessary daily exercise I used to stroll round it before breakfast.

The animals and vegetables soon got used to my presence and became quite tame. The whales would come up to the shore in the morning and eat crumbs out of my hand.

And there was a dear old octopus. I used to call "Puss, puss, puss," and it would come frisking round my feet, barking with pleasure. When the sea was calm I frequently went for a ride on this octopus, and found it splendid for the liver. Just to show how clever I became, I'm ready to back myself to give Tod Sloan or Tommy Loates a stone and a half on octopus-back over any course approved of by the Jockey Club and the Royal Humane Society. I don't say this in a boastful spirit, but just to prove to you that I'm in earnest.

Well, the years fled by and the months passed quickly away, and one week succeeded another— there isn't much difference in weeks, they all have their weekness—and about the third day of my

confinement in the neighbourhood of " The Shells"
I spied a boat hooked on the horizon. You must
understand that I had been doing my best to
attract the attention of any passing vessels or
policemen. I always left twopence on the doorstep at night for the milkman, but he never came.
And after I had finished reading my newspaper
I used to make a flag of it and fasten it to the
chimney, knowing how eager the average sensual
man is to grab a newspaper that he has not paid
for.

Well, the boat drew nearer and nearer, until at
last it ran ashore, when who should step out
but Mrs. Kelly *to be continued.*

I Strike the
Mainland

NO! it was not Mrs. Kelly, only a lady in black very like her. She was a wonderful woman. As soon as she went in my house on this desert island she started to put things straight. I was impressionable at that time, and I had stuck up over the chimney-piece about a dozen photographs of professional beauties. They were looking a bit off colour, but they cheered my lonely life. Well, as soon as this dark woman caught sight of them she pulled them down and stuffed them in the fire-grate.

"Make yourself at home," I said. "Go on with your work of destruction. If you'd like to chuck lumps of coal at the gas globes, don't mind me."

And her brother that came with her sat on the table, put his feet on the mantel-piece, lighted up my favourite pipe, and spat on the ceiling. After he was tired of that he got up and threw all the cups and saucers out of the window.

I was walking up and down like a caged lion, lashing myself into fury. Suddenly a thought struck me. I rushed out of the house, jumped into the boat and pushed off. I thought it was a fair exchange, my villa for their boat.

I put my shirt up for a sail, and I rowed as hard as I could, but I found that I made much better progress by getting out and swimming and pushing the boat with my head.

I must have gone hundreds of miles like this until one day I bumped against something soft, and saw that I had struck a chip of mainland that had been broken off. It was a very much indented shore, as creeky as new boots, and I pushed my craft up one of these creeks until I thought it was about tea-time. Then I landed and helped myself to a piece of cake that I found in the boat. There were no currants in the cake, but there were holes where the currants had been, and I rejoiced to find these traces of civilization.

Suddenly I was terrified by the spectacle of a savage chief dancing round me. He was painted red and yellow like a mixed sunset, and he wore a single eye-glass in his nose. He made a great many cursory remarks unfit for publication, and then he approached and tapped me tenderly on the cheek with his kutankumagen (this is the native word for sword).

Of course, I did not let him see that I was afraid; I asked him if I was anywhere near Liverpool. He semed affected. Large tears came to his eyes—and I ought to tell you that tears are very large in these parts in the summer months; as a rule they run three to a pint, but you can

F

have them bigger if you like. These tears chased each other down his face, which was several distances in length, and fell with heavy splashes on the ground. I was much touched.

"Weep not," I cried, "O black-eyed wanderer of the back gardens. It is peace, not pieces."

"Chuck it," said the chief. "I'm an Irishwoman and I was born in Liverpool, and the sight of your beautiful face and massive form makes me want to go home again."

As I have said, the ground was very soft, and during this little conversation we had to keep jumping about to prevent ourselves from sinking. It looked like a sort of cock fight more than anything else. My boat had sunk long ago, weighed down by the remains of my cake, and there was nothing to show for it but a clay pipe and a straw hat.

I was soon tired of dancing, but the Irish lady said she had been practising for ten years and knew all the steps.

She told me she loved me (to a dreamy waltz). But I thought, No, I haven't come down to that yet, and so I refused her (to a Highland fling). Then she got very angry (to a mixture of a tarantella and a Zulu war dance) and I tried to calm her (to a dainty gavotte). But she became more and more violent, throwing a couple of back somersaults, and telling me (to a marionette dance) that unless I gave my consent she would call her husband and have me boiled before the sunset next morning. I danced an Irish gig, and told her to go and boil herself.

At this up came her husband, and about a hundred more, executing a sort of wild barn dance. One of them, a streaky-looking gentleman with a moustache like a nail brush, suggested frying me (to a sort of toe solo), but he got his sword between his legs and fell head first into the mud.

I was getting very tired in the legs.

"How do you do when you want to go to bed on this mud?" I asked the Irishwoman.

"Oh," she said, "we never use anything but the best spring mattresses."

Well, then there was a song and chorus, which I quote from memory—

Chief.

"Behold the gooseliper
　　Sits panig in the gloot,
To await the snoosegiper,
　　Who wields the dread bazoot.

Chorus.

"Take it off his back,
　　Ta-ake i-it o-off hi-is ba-ack.

Chief.

"For the walliskange shall wardle,
　　And the philistover seek,
And black shall be the bardle
　　Of the gillysober's beak.

Chorus (still dancing).

"For we won't go home till mo-orning,
　　Till daylight doth appear."

What was I to do in such a terrible predicament?
It was a case for desperate remedies, and so I
must ask you to forgive me for what I did. It was
a cruel thing in this humanitarian age, but it had
to be.

I cleared my throat of the mud they had put
there, and in as·cold-blooded a manner as possible
I sang—
　　　　" I am but a poor blind boy."

Poor, poor creatures! Never shall I forget the
effect of that little ballad. Strong men wept like
baby elephants, and others shook from head to
face with emotion. In fact, I have never seen
anything that looked so much like anything else
I had ever seen before as this did.

Each of them looked at the other to take a last
fond farewell, and then at me in silent reproach,
and then they sank for ever in the soft ground;
and just to show what forgiveness there can be in
savage breasts they pushed my boat up for me, so
that I could start off again on my voyage.

Eventually I reached Japan, a country on which
I have since delivered lectures at meetings of the
British Association at the Tivoli, Oxford, and
Pavilion. I settled down there as a rhubarb
merchant, and the next place to mine was a
ginger - beer plantation. He was a very nice
fellow, the owner; he used to throw all the broken
bottles into my garden.

One morning, when I was weeding the glass,
I happened to look up, and there I saw a woman's

A CHAP UNEASY (JAPANESY).

head just peeping over the wall. That's the sort of thing that always moves me, but I pretended not to see, and she had to attract my attention with a loose piece of wall, and when I turned round she winked at me—with her ear, not her eye. In England the highest society wink their eye, but it would not be considered etiquette in Japan. So I walked over to her—I walked backwards to make people think I was coming away—and she invited me into the house to have a cup of Japanese delight.

I had not sat there two minutes before in came her father. To this day I believe it was a put-up job to make me look small. As soon as he saw me he pulled out a sword about two feet long and one foot broad, and said, in a nasty tone of voice, " Young man ! " It always makes my heart flutter when I hear that expression used.

Well, I looked at the man and the sword and the door, and I saw that I couldn't help it. I said, "After you, sir, with the cheese-cutter." But no, he would not be pleasant. He said, "Young man, you must marry Lung Lung at once." I said, " Is that all ? Why, I'm doing that sort of thing every day."

It was a curious ceremony: everything is so different in Japan. Fancy walking to church on your hands, with people tickling your feet all the way ; that's supposed to be a special sort of preparation for married life. Then you have to turn round three times and kiss the bride. First I turned round three times and fell into the spittoon.

Then I turned the bride round three times and kissed myself.

In Japan the girls are different—even the girls. They ask the men for presents out there, a thing unheard of in Europe. There are many other strange customs. Instead of cutting a slice of bread and scraping butter on top as we do (when we've got any), they cut the bread and put the butter underneath, and then turn it over. Here, in England, we have relations ; there, in Japan, the relations have us. That's another strange thing. Here you ring the door-bell, there you pull a handle and it's the bell that rings. English people take a cab, but in Japan the cab takes them. Yes, I knew you would say that.

However, as I daresay you know, I returned to England some years since, and I have almost become accustomed to the change.

CHAPTER
ELEVENTH

One of My
Failures

I T was in a north-country town, which I will not
specify beyond saying that it was near the
knuckle of Yorkshire. A great friend of mine—
a ballad singer with a reverberating baritone of
such power that it used to break the glasses of
the audience before they had finished their drinks,
and consequently they had to order some more and
pay for the broken glass; hence he always commanded a fairly high salary—— I don't know
where I am now. I 'll begin that sentence again.

A friend of mine—with a black beard of such
resemblance to half a yard of crape that he used
to tie a bit of it round his arm when anybody died
and get a special engagement as chief mourner—
well, to cut it short,—not the beard, but the description—he was a big, dark, solemn-looking chap who
used to have a lot to say in his songs about the
bellows' roar, and the briny sweep, and that sort
of thing.

And it happened that in this particular town
he was in great request for churchy and chapelly
shows and temperance smoking concerts, where

he used to sing "Rocked in the Cradle of the Deep" and other lively little things of that sort, with original wheezes of his own dropped in the cradle, as it were.

Now he had a very bad cold once, so bad that when he talked people would look up and down and wonder where that horrible noise came from, and, as a friend, he appealed to me to go in his place to a show called the Guild of High Endeavour.

"What is it?" I said. "A sort of shooting gallery?"

"No," he growled; "it's connected with the Congregationalist chapel. It's held once a week to keep their young people from going to the wicked theatre and music-hall."

Well, you must understand that at that time I had not evolved into what I have now become, after many years' hard labour—I mean industry, of course; and I was in embryo, so to speak—there again, of course, I mean artistically, not otherwise. (I don't like explaining everything like this, but I shouldn't like you to fall under a misapprehension and hurt yourself.)

Where was I? Oh, yes, in embryo.

Well, people in the profession didn't know then what I couldn't do, and this friend of mine asked me to go and take his place, thinking that I should do.

He said, "You know you've got a very religious face, Dan, when you're properly made up, and your feet are just the thing." He couldn't resist throwing my feet in my face.

"And there's money in it too," he said.

It tickled me. I thought I would try what I could do with this strange audience.

So after my turn at the hall, which came early in the evening, I parted my hair down the middle and put on a Shakespeare collar and a sad smile, and off I went.

You have heard of stage fright, of course? Well, when I got on the platform there I had a sort of hydrophobic attack of. it. We sat in a row, with me, as the only professional, near the chairman in the middle. Some of us were singers, some of us were story-tellers, and some of us were in the last stages of recitationitis.

And the gloom was as thick as pea-soup.

The chairman was a parson with a face like a suet pudding that had fallen on a door-mat and picked up some whiskers. He made a long speech about this Guild of High Endeavour, and said that they were going to listen to something which would help them on the right path and comfort them in the tribulations which the righteous suffer in this world.

Fancy me doing a turn like that!

I thought to myself, "They'll kill me when I start." I was trembling all over, and I had not even the nerve to get up and rush off the platform, because it was a long way to the door, and I should have to pass by the whole audience.

At last it came to my turn.

"Mr. Daniel Leno," said the chairman, "a brand, may I say, plucked from the burning, will now sing that beautiful tone-picture, "The Lost Chord.""

He did not stop there.   He could not leave it.

"And oh!" he went on, "let us trust, my friends, that some of us may find that chord to-night," and a good deal more to the same effect, which I was too paralysed to remember.   I only hoped he would keep it up for a few hours.

But it came to an end, and somebody put a sheet of music into my hand.   My heart had been in my boots for a long time, and I looked down to stop it from rolling off the platform, if it should go any further.

Then I cleared my voice with such a heart-rending sob that the audience became uneasy.

The pianist started the accompaniment, and the dreadful moment rapidly approached when all these good people would get up and throw the pews at me.   I coughed again and started—you remember the lines—

"Seated one day at the organ," etc.

Well, you know how the song goes, and you know what sort of a voice I have, and so you can imagine that "The Lost Chord" was sung that night as it never was sung before.

I was in a cold perspiration, and I never raised my eyes, but went steadily on with the first verse, in spite of curious noises amongst the audience.

Then, when I came to a rest, I ventured to peep round the edge of the sheet of music.

What a sight!

The chairman had his elbows on the table, and he was holding his jaws hard with both hands.

Some of the stern-faced men in front of me had their lips tightly closed and were shaking in their seats like jellies. Some of the women were trying to chew their pocket-handkerchiefs. There was a general air of uneasiness in the place.

"Well," I thought, "I'm not dead yet. I'll let 'em have the rest straight from the heart."

So I lowered the music sheet and sang with all the expression I could possibly put into the sad words of my song. I threw in a tough bit of passionate yearning in the last few words, and that settled them altogether. One old churchwarden was polite enough to get up and run out down the aisle, cuddling himself; but the rest—they simply broke down utterly, and roared and screamed like children. I don't suppose there ever was such a noise in that building before. The chairman that called me a brand from the burning was sputtering and wiping his eyes. He was almost in a hysterical condition.

I said to him, "This isn't a comic song; you said I was to sing 'The Lost Chord,' and I did. What is there to laugh at?"

When the people's faces got a bit straight again they rewarded me for my exertions with vigorous applause; but I refused an encore. I felt annoyed at having been placed in a false position, as it were.

And I have never sung for the Guild of High Endeavour since. I wonder if any of the members ever came to the wicked music-hall on the off chance of hearing me repeat my wonderful success with "The Lost Chord"?

CHAPTER   *Chronological*
TWELFTH   *Explanations*

I DÒN'T like talking about myself; that's why
I'm writing this book. But my publisher
keeps telling me that it ought to be more of
a naughty biography than a collection of dis-
connected reminiscences.

Well, to get it over, I think I told you that I
toured all over the three kingdoms, as well as
part of Germany, with my parents. I first made
a separate reputation for myself at Dublin. One·
week I was singing at the smallest hall in the
town at 15*s.* a week, and the next I was engaged
at the Exhibition Palace for £1 15*s.* a night,
which was a very pleasant change, I can assure
you. I became well known in Ireland, and at
Belfast I had the honour to receive a high com-
pliment from Charles Dickens, who saw me at
the time he was lecturing there.

All this time I kept on practising dancing,
which is one of the most exacting of arts. In
1880 my father saw an advertisement in the
Era announcing a clog-dancing competition at
Leeds for the championship of the world, and

Yours truly,
Dan Leno
1897

on his advice I entered, but I had no expectation of winning.

However, after dancing against seventeen of the finest performers in the profession, the judges awarded me the championship belt, and I held my title in three more competitions.

I have been working hard all my life since I was three, but about this time I think I did more than ever before or since. Sometimes our family party nearly filled the entire programme. We have appeared on the bills as " The Leno Family," " Mr. and Mrs. Leno," " The Brothers Leno," and " Dan Leno."

In a few years I was able to allow my parents to retire on a comfortable pension, and then I got married to Miss Lydia Reynolds.

I started on the conquest of London by singing at three halls, the Foresters', Middlesex, and Gatti's, with songs and dances. My first great success in the song line was a charming little ballad called " Milk for the Twins," for which I was disguised as a distressed female. Because Mr. George Conquest saw me in this costume I was engaged to play old women in pantomimes for some years after, my first part being Jack's mother in *Jack and the Beanstalk* at the Surrey Theatre in 1886. Next year I reappeared there in *Sinbad*, and then I was engaged by Sir Augustus Harris for Drury Lane as the Baroness in *Babes in the Wood.* The company was a strong one, including Harriet Vernon, Florence Dysart, Maggie Duggan, my wife Lydia

Dear Sir

I hereby agree to lay down Mrs Lens

For 6 acres to steam up the Hospital Gardens
Norwich to commence 12/4/1884

£ 1201.0.0. 30.. to lay d 12 Horse Power
and fit in the works Bylow Gate with motor
for Bill and usual lot 3..... Sold Pramiture B Bt
..... Eighth .....

Hospital Gardens
George .....

March 1/84

A FAC-SIMILE OF ONE OF MY CONTRACTS.

Reynolds, Sybil Grey, Rose Deering, Harry Nicholls, Herbert Campbell, Victor Stevens, Tom Pleon, Charles Lauri, Walter Andrews, Dezano, Reuben Inch, and the Brothers Griffiths.

Since then I have played in *Jack and the Beanstalk* (1889), *Beauty and the Beast* (1890), *Humpty Dumpty* (1891), *Little Bo-peep* (1892), *Robinson Crusoe* (1893), *Whittington and his Cat* (1894), *Cinderella* (1895), *Aladdin* (1896), and *Babes in the Wood* (1897).

And now I have thrown these autobiographical details off my chest let us continue our game.

DAN LENO
AS
THE
WIDOW
TWANKEY

CHAPTER   *Among My*
THIRTEENTH   *Books*

I HASTEN to explain that I am referring to the less-known kind of books. I am not much of a betting man, and I never know which is the best horse in a race until I see the numbers up.

I am a great lover of the classics, and I have got a good many wheezes out of old authors like Shakespeare and Walter Scott and Marie Corelli. When I read the *Sorrows of Satan*, for instance, I struck the book with the flat of my fist, and I said, "Now that's a part I should like to play!" Dan Leno as Satan, with a pretty little song and a dance to finish with; a sort of double shuffle it would have to be, to suit the character.

Of course, as you know, I played Hamlet at Drury Lane last Christmas; and when I remembered that Garrick and Kean and a lot of other eccentric comedians had done the same thing in the same place, I had a sort of yearning to know whether they would think mine was as funny as theirs. Some day I'm going to tackle Macbeth, with Herbert Campbell as Lady Mac.

It ought to be a bit blood-curdling with a safe man at the limelight.

Yes, I congratulate myself that I have done something to bring about the romantic revival. I believe in romance. I ought, by rights, to have been born in the Middle Ages, and gone touring with the crusaders to Joppa and Jericho for six nights only.

Nowadays there is no romance: girls marry anybody they like.

Suppose—just to take an example—I don't mean that I know the girl—suppose a haughty damsel fell in love, as it were, with a plumber's apprentice, come to put a pane of glass in the baronial hall that her father had broken with his swollen head, through attempting to get in at three o'clock that morning without disturbing the household.

Well, you know what would have happened in the good old times. The old man would have at once sent a wire to a good band of assassins —I don't mean a street corner band—to come and slit the plumber's larynx or weasand, and lock up his daughter in a lonely tower on a glass of milk and a mixed biscuit. That's romance.

There's just a chance that the plumber might go abroad and come back from Klondike disguised as a wandering minstrel, but he couldn't be sure that the girl would be still there; she might be married to some old-established knight with a good pitch in the neighbourhood.

It's altogether different now. The old man
can't go to the stores and ask to see a few nice

DAN LENO
AS
HAMLET

ALAS!
POOR
YORICK

assassins to choose from, and the girl will pretty
soon shut him up if he attempts to be firm. Why
even supposing he disowned her, she could get

a good engagement at the halls singing duets
with the plumber. That's business!

Then there are no proper elopements now.
When you see the word "elopement" in the
evening paper you know what it is. Mrs. Brown,
the porkmonger's wife, has run away with Mr.
Jones, the scissors-grinder, and they're up before
the magistrate because she took the family hatchet
with her in case it might be required.

That is why I like novels to be about the good
old days. Some day when I have half an hour to
spare I am going to write a historical novel myself.
I have been approached by a publisher already.
His first remark struck me forcibly; he said,
"What'll you have?"

Then when I had had, he went on to propose
that I should write a romance of the period of
the Ancient Britons. He said they'd never been
done, and I remarked that they must have been
sharper than their descendants.

But I explained to him that I wanted a grander
scheme. I want to introduce a lot of historical
characters into the book—Julius Cæsar and Marie
Lloyd. and the Duke of Wellington. I should
like to put in a chapter of dialogue between
Henry VIII. and Mrs. Ormiston Chant. The
publisher thought it was a good idea, but he
said it would be difficult to find a *milieu*.

So I saw he was backing out of the business
when he began talking French. I am not much
of a linguist, and that's why I can't tell you

anything about Scotch novels until they are
published in an English translation.

I don't know whether you have ever heard of
Isaac Watts. He is a great favourite of mine.
He wrote a lot of good comic songs, and the only
thing to regret is that his patter has not been
handed down to us. Then there's Young's *Night
Thoughts*. Poor old Young! There's a lot of ·
moonshine in *Night Thoughts;* but if he'd been
going round the town now with some people I
know he wouldn't have had any night thoughts
the next morning.

I am never tired of reading *Paradise ˙ Lost*.
Perhaps that's because I never start on it; but
I really must say I think it is one of Dickens's
failures. His judgment was at fault when he
wrote it. For a purely lyric poet like him to set
out to write a twelve-act comedy-of-manners seems
to me to have been rash and ill-considered. He
ought to have followed the example of his bosom
friend Pope, and confined himself to conundrums.

Yes, I'm very fond of classical literature, and
there is one classical writer I particularly admire,
though he does not seem to be generally recognized by classical scholars and other old fogies.
His name is Saul Smiff, and he wrote a very
learned treatise, called *The Pottle Papers*. I read
The Pottle Papers and enjoyed them loudly.

Indeed, I have not been so much interested in
anything since I learned Foxe's *Book of " To-
martyrs"* off by heart while studying the historical

relations of the Tower of London and the London
Pavilion. The only thing I am sorry for is that
I didn't know Pottle sooner. If that book had
been put into my hands when I was, about three
months old it might have influenced my whole
career. It would have enlivened many a weary
hour and kept me from the bottle. As it was
I had to put up with literature of the flimsiest
description. Pottle is a man I should like to play
football with.

What is this thin volume I pull from the shelf?
Poetry, I suppose. No—— what's this? Nine
shirts. I'm sure I haven't had nine shirts washed
this week. And just fancy people sticking the
washing book in my library between two new
novels. It ought to be next to the Bible.

I bought a little while since a book called *The
Canterbury Tales*, by a Mr. Geoffrey Chaucer, and
it just shows what humbugs these authors are. I
assure you that the stories in the book have
nothing whatever to do with the Canterbury. Mr.
Adney Payne was very much annoyed when I
told him, to think that his favourite hall should be
used to advertise a work of this kind by an un-
scrupulous catch-penny author. Payne thinks this
Mr. Chaucer is a disappointed artist who wanted
to take his trousers off while swinging from a
trapeze, but could not get an engagement, naturally,
because that sort of performance is only suitable
for a lady, and even then it should be at a West-
end hall.

Moreover, the stories are so scandalously shocking that when we read them the second time Payne and I could not help blushing, and we wondered what the County Council was doing to allow it.

A healthy, moral tone should always be observed. I was very pleased, not long ago, when I went into a very cheap music-hall in the suburbs to see a line on the programme earnestly requesting the audience to complain at once if they noticed any absence of impropriety in the performance. It may have been a misprint, but it was well meant.

CHAPTER
FOURTEENTH

A Little Music

I AM to a great extent a self-educated man, and I have tackled nearly all the arts and sciences in a sixpenny sort of way.

But in the whole course of my studies I never had such an exciting time as when I tried to obtain complete mastery of the bagpipes in seven lessons without a master. I was not particularly fond of the instrument, and I think I can understand why it is rarely played at symphony concerts. But I had an absorbing curiosity to find out whether I could produce a pathetic effect by squealing the "Maiden's Prayer" on it. I thought it would be the most touching musical performance ever known.

My landlady at that time was a well-nourished female, but she had no ear; she had to listen through her nose, and that of course gave her a prejudice against classical music.

My first attempt was startling. I had shut the door and taken a large mouthful of the pipes, and after blowing away until my teeth nearly dropped out I managed to fill the bag or cistern with several gallons of south-west wind.

Nothing happened for a few minutes; but just as I was panting and sighing before starting again the instrument seemed to wake up suddenly to a sense of its surroundings, and started screaming and wailing and spitting. It sounded like thirty cats with their tails in a mangle.

I dropped the thing in terror and rushed from the room.

On the landing I met my landlady, who took me tenderly in her arms, and kissing me softly on the forehead, asked me where the pain was, and told me her husband used to suffer in the same way, but she didn't think he ever had it as bad as I had.

The young man who lived above me was a powerful and generally ill-natured fellow; but on this occasion he took it very gently, and I was greatly relieved when he sent word down to ask if Mr. Leno would kindly leave off singing, as he wanted to go to sleep.

On the occasion of my second lesson I began to practise in my bedroom before breakfast, and I saw through the window a dear old heavy-weight friend of mine coming along to invite himself to breakfast.

I blew hard into the reservoir, and then I put the instrument under the bed-clothes and awaited my visitor.

"Hello, old man!" said the hearty guest, "up already? More study? Never mind a chair, I'll sit on the washstand."

That wasn't what I wanted, so I immediately flooded the washstand by upsetting some water.

"Well, then, I'll sit on the bed," he cried.

He sat on the bed—flopped down on it in his jolly way.

My bagpipes rose nobly to the occasion. As soon as my friend's trunk came in contact with the bed there was an outburst of blood-curdling groans and shrieks from under the clothes. It was a really frightful noise that made even my heart stand still.

My friend leaped so high that he bumped his head against the ceiling. His hair stood on end, his teeth rattled, his knees knocked together.

"Good God, Dan!" he chattered, "I must have ki—ki—killed the child."

I never saw such a picture of tragic horror in my life.

Suddenly he seemed to recover the use of his limbs; he opened the door and dashed wildly into the street.

I shouted out to him through the window. I said, "It's no use running away; we must face this catastrophe and decide what to do. Come up at once. If people see you like that they'll begin to suspect something."

So he came back trembling, and I began seriously to discuss with him the advisability of hiding the body under the floor, and then emigrating to Venezuela.

His face was buried in his hands, and he

seemed dazed with the thought that his career was blighted.

Then he rose up with calm resolution on his countenance. He approached the bed and gently touched the cover.

The pipes uttered a funny little sigh.

"Dan!" sobbed my heavy friend, "it still lives! it still lives!"

Then he turned down the bed-clothes.

CURTAIN.

No—I can't describe that scene. There is no known language on earth that would do for it. You must imagine it for yourself.

* * * * *

Do you know how to play the musical basins? That's another nice instrument.

A friend of mine composed a touching ballad, entitled "Let it alone or you'll break it," and I thought I would practise it on the basins and reveal new beauties to him when I had learned to play it.

Well, first of all you go to the City and take out an accident insurance policy. Then you get about twenty white pot basins—the colour makes a lot of difference—and tune them by injecting water in them with a squirt to various levels, until they sound the right note.

N.B.—You should have rather a large squirt, it comes in handy to protect the musician from personal violence from critics.

When you have got the basins all in tune to the extent of a couple of octaves you glue your music on the face of the best looking-glass—the musical basins are a drawing-room instrument, of course— and then you take up a sixteen-ounce hammer in each hand—some players spit on their hands first, but I don't think that affects the tone at all—and strike the basins.

The harder you hit the louder the music—up to a certain point, where music leaves off and a cinematograph of Niagara begins. I have learned to play the first four bars of the melody, and I have only broken twelve basins and saturated the best carpet. A good deal of the sound escaped through the flooring and pattered into the room below.

But this is nothing, I am only practising the air now. Wait till I attack the accompaniment.

CHAPTER FIFTEENTH

How to be Married though Happy

ANYBODY who takes no interest in the subject need not read this chapter. I won't make him. But I have some burning thoughts about marriage which must come out. I know there are a great number of young men about who are wanting not to get—— I mean wanting to get married, and I'm going to give them a few words of comfort.

Now, in my opinion the present system of starting the show is all wrong. It is generally thought that when a man wants to get married the first thing necessary is some sort of a woman. You may get a patent woman, or only a colourable infringement, but something of the kind is thought necessary.

But I maintain that this is beginning at the wrong end altogether. The girl should be the last thing, the final touch as it were.

First of all, I say, let the man count his money, and make a rough estimate of his prospects with the aid of a ready reckoner and the latest betting news. Then he can draw up a sort of balance-sheet (I consulted a chartered accountant on this question, who guided my hand), and he sticks the proposed wife down there in two parts: on one side as an asset, and on the other as a liability. Of course, it's guess-work mostly; some wives are all on one side or the other, but most of them you don't know which.

Then, if he decides to go on with the business, he should take a lot of preliminary precautions; don't let him run off at once and look round for a small or large girl. Not at all.

Let him take a house in a neighbourhood that he prefers, and let him furnish it throughout, according to his own taste and pocket, and live there. Let him choose his own servant or servants, again to taste; and then, if he thinks the show incomplete, and perseveres in his intention of marrying, which is doubtful, he must go out to the marriage market and see what's going on.

The advantages of this method must be obvious to the most powerful intellect. You see it stumps the girl at once. In other words, she is confronted with a *fait accompli*, an accomplished fact that can vamp and speak several languages.

If she says she wants to live at Hampstead, he replies that he has taken a house at Brixton on a seven years' lease, and she will be foiled in her schemes for walking him round the furniture shops and ruining him in sideboards and suites.

Now comes the question of the question.

ME !

H

I have had a lot of experience. Between the ages of six and nineteen I was rejected eleven times and accepted fifteen times, so that I consider myself an expert.

Lately there has been a change in proposal fashions. Formerly the poor chap would sit at one side of the room and the girl at the other, both suffering from cold feet, and he would stammer :

"Miss Jenkins—er—I have—er—I have something—very serious. I——"

And the girl would be careful to reply in a tone that would not compromise her :

"Oh, I'm so sorry to hear that. Why don't you go and see a doctor at once? Aren't you taking anything for it ? "

Then the young man would be shut up, and would go away for a fortnight to think out a more brilliant scheme.

Back he comes full of hopes and fears, and probably half full of ginger beer, lemonade, and all kinds of refreshments. And he sits on the edge of a chair again and gurgles :

"Miss Jenkins—er—may I—oh, may I call you Madeline ? "

Then of course the girl would be overwhelmed with confusion and astonishment, and would have to get up and stroll in front of the looking-glass to see what had produced this outburst, so that she could try it on somebody else.

After making a note of it she would wipe the

powder off with her handkerchief to give her best blush a chance, and she would cast her eyes down on the hearth-rug. (I don't mean she would actually do that, only figuratively—she wants her eyes for the following scenes.)

At last the trembling young suitor would be treated to the startlingly original remark:

"But, Mr. Binns — this — this is so sudden. I never dreamt——" Although she has, of course, been wondering for three months how long the fellow would take to make up his mind.

I think that the "sudden" business has gone out of fashion lately. It doesn't seem to work, and the girls have dropped it.

I remember a young friend telling me that no sooner had his future pronounced the word "sudden" than the whole of her mother rushed into the room and embraced him with tears, and she was immediately followed by the rest of the family, who wanted to borrow five shillings each, so that the girl was rather embarrassed, and the young man felt as if he had just got up after an earthquake.

Fortunately the formal proposal has gone out. The parties meet each other half way, or at a dark corner, or under a gas lamp, and after a little conversation about the weather and each other's relations they glide into one another's affections, or chuck themselves in, according to temperament and the season of the year.

You take a beautiful moonlight walk, say, in

April, and the girl nestles against your ribs and looks up at the moon, and says in a wistful manner :

"George, don't you think June is the best month of the whole year for getting married? I'm always going to be married in June."

And you turn your head away and murmur "Dam!" down your coat sleeve.

Then you pull yourself together—she'll help—and you say desperately :

"Oh, I don't know; one month's as good as another, except that the month after next is better than the next!"

"Oh, well," she replies, "if you prefer May——"

And there you are.

I believe there are few "May I call you Madeline?" cases nowadays. The man that has to ask such an appalling question has either been wooing an icebergess, or he has not a 66 to 1 chance.

Anyhow, he might as well call her Madeline without asking and see how she takes it; apologies are cheap enough, and she won't think any the worse of him.

CHAPTER SIXTEENTH   *A Baby Story*

A CURIOUS incident happened to a young conjurer that I used to know. He was a very gallant man, and had sweethearts in every town, whose acquaintance he had made in different ways.

This was in Manchester, where the adventure took place. My friend—I'll call him Floro, as I daren't give him his real name, he might change me to a rabbit or a bunch of geraniums—was strolling along a street in a busy part of the town when he saw a comely damsel struggling with a white bundle in her arms.

This was the sort of thing Floro was great in.

"Let me carry that for you," he said, in that graceful, knightly, irresistible, got-to-have-me way of his.

Well, the girl looked at him queerly and then plumped the bundle in his arms.

"Oh, but I didn't know it was a ba——" he stammered.

"Now do hold him up!" appealed the girl. "I was so tired, and I'm so glad I met you."

It was just then that I happened to come along. Knowing that Floro was married to a lady at Brixton I was naturally shocked at the spectacle, and I put my handkerchief up to hide my face and disguise my feelings; but it was no use, he recognized me.

"I say, Leno," he cried, "you know more about these things than I do. Catch hold of this."

"No," I replied sternly, "I refuse to take it off your hands; all I'll do is to walk behind and look on. It's your child, not mine." ·

"No, it isn't mine either; it belongs to this young lady."

"Nothing of the kind," said the girl; "how dare you say such a thing? Mine, indeed! Why, I never saw it before in all my life."

Floro's eyes stared wide open with horror.

"Wh—a—at!" he gasped; "wh—y—why—Oh, Lord, here's a nice mess!"

He raised the bundle and used it to wipe the gathering perspiration from his crimson brow.

"I say, Leno, old man, do see me through with this, won't you?" he implored; "it's a deliberate plant. I assure you I never saw the dam kid before."

"Well, what are you doing with it then?" I asked.

"I don't know," said the conjurer; "there's no deception — I mean I'm not humbugging you, really. Come on, we mustn't lose sight of her."

"Don't you follow me!" snapped the girl;

"don't you dare! I'm going in here to buy some safety pins, and if you come after me I'll call a policeman."

I think I ought to tell you before we go any further that the whole business was a practical joke, and that I and the little lady were acting in collusion to take a rise out of Floro. The baby, moreover, was only a property baby.

But I really pitied the unfortunate conjurer with this addition to his family suddenly thrust upon him.

"This'll drive me off my chump," he cried in accents of agony. "Come on; I'm going after her."

It was a large store, one of the sort where you can buy anything from a halfpenny-worth of tea and sugar mixed to a furnished house with a ready-made family in it.

My poor persecuted, perspiring friend stepped in and accosted a bland and well-buttered shop-walker, who was pacing the floor and rubbing his hands.

"I say," said Floro, "which is the way to the— safety-pin department?" I am clearing out his frequent expletives.

Well, the shopwalker had had a lot of practice in keeping a straight face, but the sight of a fashionably dressed gentleman awkwardly carrying a baby and asking for the safety-pin department hit him right on his diaphragm, and he had to turn round and laugh softly for a few seconds.

At the same time one of the young men of the shop ducked below the counter, making a noise like tearing calico.

Floro was blushing like a furnace, and cursing under his breath.

" Upstairs, sir, turn to your left," said the shop-walker. Then he shouted with tears in his voice, " Forward! safety pins for this gentleman."

Unfortunately, just when Floro had got half-way up the staircase the baby seemed to hit him in the eye, as if it had had enough of this treatment. Perhaps he was trying some new juggling idea with it. Anyhow, it dipped under his arm and rolled to the bottom with frightful velocity, bouncing off each step as it came.

You should have seen that sight; it was thrilling! The shopwalker, two or three countermen, and seven or eight female customers dashed at the property baby, uttering cries of horror and pity.

It was like a furious football scrimmage. The shopwalker got there first and tossed the baby in the air, passing it to a robust matron, who started on a sprint for a chair and scored a touch-down.

" Poor thing," cried the matron, with a sym-pathetic crowd round her, " poor — poor little thing. There, there, there, and such a quiet little thing too."

" Oh, do let me look at its face," said a younger woman.

Well, the fact is the thing hadn't got any face. They uncovered one end, and then they turned the poor little thing upside down and uncovered the other end.

Their faces!—it was worth fifty pounds to look at them.

I was doing a quiet little soft shoe dance in a corner and humming with joy. It was one of the happiest moments of my life.

Floro, of course, had fled as soon as he dropped the baby—fled feeling that he had committed a terrible crime, and I daren't go and claim the poor little thing until the crowd simmered down a bit.

Presently I was able to explain things to the shopwalker, and I scuttled out of the shop with the bundle under my arm.

When I saw Floro that night I hurried to let him know all the details before his turn, because the poor fellow could not have juggled very cleverly with that crime on his conscience.

He was looking very sad and frightened through his make-up, and he almost fell on my neck.

"Was the kid hurt?" he cried hoarsely.

"No," I said.

"Thank God!" And after this pious exclamation he continued, "Well, I think we got out of that mess very nicely. Where did it get to ultimately? But I don't care so long as I shall never see it again."

"You will though," I said; "I've got it here."

He sank speechless into the nearest seat, wringing his hands.

" Here it is," I cried, flinging it on the floor with all my strength.

It took him a few minutes to decide whether to knock my brains out or not ; but at last he burst into a fit of hysterical laughing, and the tears rolled down his painted face, leaving tram lines behind them.

And his performance went splendidly that night.

*   *   *   *   *

That reminds me of something else which has nothing at all to do with it.

A touring melodrama company required a little girl of about seven to come on in a most thrilling situation and cry, " Oh, my sister!" when she saw the heroine in a position of frightful danger owing to the machinations of the chief villain. She had nothing else to do in the play but say " Oh, my sister!" in a surprised tone of voice; but it required careful rehearsing.

They used to hire a girl in each town for the purpose, as they did not think it worth while to take one on tour, and every Monday the manager had to rehearse the scene.

One child could not utter the speech as he wanted it. She spoke it in a matter-of-fact tone, which would not do at all.

"Not like that," cried. the manager. " Look here, if you saw a plum pudding coming on for you, you wouldn't whisper ' Oh, plum pudding '

as if you didn't care a curse one way or the
other. You'd say, 'Oh, there's a dodgasted
plum pudding!' now, wouldn't you?"

"Yes, sir," murmured the child, carried away
by the vehemence and earnestness of the big
man.

"Very well, then, that's how I want you to
say it."

Well, the night came, and in the middle of the
play the heroine was fast bound by the villain to
a sort of water-mill, which was to settle her for
ever and leave him master of much gold. Ha!
ha!

The band played wobbly slow music, and the
audience held its breath, except to shout "Sit
down in front, yer fathead."

In came the little girl, took the centre of the
floor, turned, and faced the audience, and in the
usual manner of a child "speaking a piece" yelled
out:

"Oh, there's my dódgasted plum pudden!"

CHAPTER SEVENTEENTH

How I Study

I DARESAY you have noticed that in all the characters impersonated I get as near Nature as possible. I might be tempted to make them exaggerated and grotesque, but no!—I am determined to walk arm in arm with truth, whatever I do, and hold the glass up to Nature. Whether she takes ale, wine, or spirits, it's all the same to me.

And I am always careful to have my costumes absolutely correct in every detail. Mr. Alma Ta——, but I won't mention any names—enough to say that I consult all the best authorities and ransack all the old rag shops to dress my parts properly.

I study the characters themselves from the life —not still life, but sparkling life.

For instance—

When I was going to act the part of a shop-walker, I pursued this gentle animal to his lair and watched all his curious little antics.

The one I studied specially was a tall, middle-aged man, who seemed to be suffering from corns.

He walked on his heels, limping with both feet, and looked as if he would like to take his boots off and carry them in his hands as he went about his business.

So when I came in, and he said " Step this way," I tried to step his way, as if I had cornful toes, but it took a lot of practice, and before I had quite finished my studies up and down the floor a com- missionaire put his hand on my shoulder and said, in a persuasive voice, " Now then, outside."

" Not at all," I said; " he told me to step this way, and I'm trying as hard as I can. Every- body else he asks passes him by with contempt. I'm the only man in the crowd that has a go at it."

But he was rude enough to insist on my con- tinuing my studies on the pavement, and I don't pretend to be a pavement artist.

Also when I was trying to get inside the character of the recruiting-sergeant I spent a lot of time round by the National Gallery.

I saw the soldiers go up and accost likely young men, and I tried to imitate them.

In order not to give myself away I tied a bit of string to a five-shilling piece and hung it round my neck, so that it stuck on my breast like a medal. There wasn't another medal there half the size of mine, and I felt a new man with it on.

I had a little cane in my hand like the others, and when I caught sight of a fellow's back who

was reading the poster about the advantages of
the army, I whacked him with the cane and said:
"Now, my lad, thinking of joining the service?"

At least that was what I intended to say, but
when I hit him he turned round, and I saw that
he was a red-faced gentleman of about forty-five,
dressed in his best.

"God bless my soul!" he muttered when he
saw me. "Who are you, and where did you get
that extraordinary medal on your chest? Are
you really one of England's soldiers?"

"Yes," I said.

"My poor country," groaned the gentleman;
"what's to become of England?"

"You leave that to me," I said; "I'll look after
that."

"And have you seen much service, my man?"

"Service!" I replied with a spice of scorn in my
tone, "Service! I should rather think so; I was
Wolseley's right-hand man at Tel-el-Keepbeer. He
said to me, he said, 'Look here, Dan, you know
more about this business than I do; I can't make
up my mind whether to order a charge of heavy
artillery or make the hussars and lancers form
square and advance slowly to cover their own
retreat.' So I said, 'Garnet, my boy——'"

But the man had not waited to hear the finish,
and I saw him a little way off talking earnestly
with a big soldier, both of them looking at me, so
I went round the corner to see the pictures.

When I undertook the part of a waiter, which

Mr. DAN LENO.

WITH SOLDIERS LIKE THIS TO FALL BACK UPON, ENGLAND WILL
NEVER BE IN DANGER.

was one of my most successful character delineations, I was able to study the subject thoroughly. I was fortunate enough to obtain an engagement at a middle-class restaurant as a waiter, to go one day on trial.

About twelve o'clock the fun began. My first customer was a snappish old gentleman, and I tried to calm him by smiling at him one of my best smiles.

"Fine day, sir," I said, handing him the bill of fare.

He grunted something like "Hrum! Hrum!"

Then I said, "What would you like, sir? We have some very nice strawberries and mashed, or sausage and cream—very pleasant in this hot weather—or a grilled lobster and pickled onions."

I went on chatting to him like this while he was making up his mind. He treated me most rudely, never listening to my remarks, and grunting from time to time.

"Bring me a steak and tomatoes," he growled.

I raised my apron to my eyes and wiped away a tear.

"Don't say tomatoes," I sobbed, "you don't know how it affects me when I hear that word."

"What the——"

"Ah, sir, you don't know; I had a favourite grandfather, once removed——"

"Dam good thing too," muttered the customer.

"And he suffered agonies from gout, sir—killed him at last, and we always called him a toe-martyr."

MYSELF BEING TIPPED.

(Oh, the tippy of it!)

"Get out, you blubbering idiot," yelled the man.
So I went to order his lunch.

"How long is the steak going to be?" he snarled
when I approached him again.

"Oh," I replied, getting a bit of my own back,
"it'll be about four inches."

"Gr-r-r-r," he growled, clutching a handful of
tablecloth.

I didn't worry him any more.   He looked
dangerous.

Another customer complained that he missed
his cheese.

"I'm sure I brought it," I said to him; "you
ought to keep a sharp eye on your cheese, sir.
Of course I know it's their fault really.   I'm
always telling them to put a string round its neck
and tie it up to the plate; but they're so old-
fashioned.   Take a walk round, sir, and you may
meet it."

"Very likely," he said.   "Give me my bill."

"Yes, sir.   Chop, potatoes, rice pudding, three
and nine; no bread a penny, three and ten; cigar
you didn't have, sixpence, four and four, H'm, h'm,
six and twopence."

"Not it," he protested.

"Oh, no," I corrected myself; "I forgot, you
didn't have any butter, that's seven and fourpence
—I mean four and fourpence, of course."

Another man ordered '64 port and spring
chicken, and when he got it he complained about
both of them.

I couldn't help smiling.

" I see what it is, sir. You've got the spring port and the '64 chicken—same thing, only the other way round. Pure luck, you know, pure luck. You never know how these things turn out."

" I'll know how you'll turn out," he said determinedly; " I shall see the manager about this."

But I didn't care. Two lovely young creatures had just come in, and I left everybody to attend to them.

" I don't want much," said the dark one.

" No, of course not," I murmured, with a smile of admiration.

" And I don't seem to want anything at all," said the fair one.

But they kept me very busy for the next half-hour.

Darkey finished up by ordering a toasted scone and a glass of milk.

" A coasted stone ?—yes," I said, " but take my advice, not milk."

" Isn't it good to-day ?" she asked, with a shade of anxiety in her lovely eyes.

I leaned my elbows on the table and crossed my legs gracefully, as I started to argue the question.

But just then another waiter fell over me. He had three plates of soup in one hand, several cuts off joints in the other, and miscellaneous puddings and vegetables hanging like festoons about his person.

They all rolled down my graceful attitude, and there was great confusion for two or three minutes. I pulled off a tablecloth and gave myself a hurried rub down. Then I turned again to my beautiful customers. I switched on my smile again, although I could feel the soup trickling down my back.

"No, not milk," I said; "it wouldn't sit still on top of what you've had, and I've spent one of the happiest half-hours of my life bringing you sausages and things. Don't let a glass of milk come between us. Mind your dear little digestion; for my sake, do. Let me get you a liqueur of lager."

The girls looked at each other and burst out laughing. I felt that I was getting on.

But just then somebody gripped me by the collar, and I heard the manager saying sternly:

"Look here, you get out of this right away, d'ye hear?"

The true, conscientious artist has to suffer much pain and humiliation.

CHAPTER EIGHTEENTH   *The Last Turn*

LOOKING at the mysteries of time and space from a ten minutes' turn point of view, it seems to me that what man wants is more— well, more, in fact, of whatever he has managed to get born with and picked up or dropped since. I have only met one man in my life who was perfectly satisfied with life, and he was always half drunk, and generally one and a half drunk.

The Leno System of Philosophy regards the world as a football, kicked about by higher powers, with me somewhere hanging on to the stitching by my teeth and toe-nails.

Even when I have a pipe of Craven mixture, fresh from Wardour Street, with Mr. Carreras's blessing, I do not enjoy myself as much as I deserve, although I share the opinion of Mr. J. M. Barrie as to the sublime smokableness of this "Arcadian" blend, spoken of so favourably in his popular book *My Lady Nicotine*. When I study Shakespearean *rôles* I always smoke "Craven." Yea, verily! that's why I played *Hamlet* so well. But just wait for my next triumph in a Shakespearean part. I'm going to combine the characters of Macbeth, Romeo, Othello, and Julius Cæsar. I expect I shall create a sensation.

The most intellectual and virtuous men in the world, whether they be prime ministers or bishops or actor-managers, feel sometimes a bit unchirpy, so to speak, in their sober intervals. I myself, as you will have noticed from my Tivolian lectures, am somewhat of a pessimist.

And it is not to be wondered at after all I have been through.

I remember once, when I was taking a holiday, I induced a comedian friend of mine to black his face, put on an old suit of clothes, and go round with me to the theatres before the doors opened, to see how many coppers we could get.

I did the same. I put on a dress coat, a mild red and blue fancy waistcoat, stout stockings, bitter knickerbockers, and two very old boots, one black and the other tan, and on my head I wore a pink jockey cap.

I thought we should have some real amusement, and at the same time be able to do some character studying.

But Bob—(that's not his real name)—Bob gave me palpitations when he turned up to meet me at the corner of Wellington Street. I had been waiting there about ten minutes with my tambourine shivering in my hand with nervousness, and wondering why I was ever born.

Suddenly I saw a great crowd coming over

MYSELF BUSTED.

(Tony Carter, *Sculptor*.)

Waterloo Bridge, and in the middle my friend Bob.

When I saw him I was paralysed. On his head he wore a bucket upside down, with the handle resting on his chin. Instead of a coat he was wearing a pair of white trousers like a sort of zouave jacket, with his arms stuck through the legs. Then underneath that he had on a bright yellow silk pair of old corsets that he had picked up at some rag shop. They would not meet anywhere near the middle, and revealed a crinkly mass of old newspaper at the bursting point. Round his waist was a rope from which dangled a cheap alarm clock that he wound up from time to time with graceful nonchalance. On one leg was a trouser carefully turned up at the bottom, while on the other leg was half a kilt of a lurid check pattern. He was wearing pink tights underneath, and the kilted leg ended in a little white baby sock and a dancing shoe, while on the other foot he had a monstrous boot stuffed with straw which was pushing through several large splits.

As soon as I got over my first shock I fled.

I darted between two omnibuses just as I heard his shout of joyful recognition, and without looking back I dashed up towards Covent Garden, with Bob in full pursuit. Tied up as he was I have no doubt I should have got clear away, only in turning a corner I happened to butt my head into a big policeman's belt, and the officer and I, embracing each other, rolled into the gutter.

When he recovered his breath he took a firmer grip of my collar.

"Where are you running so fast, young man?" he growled. "Stand back there——," addressing the crowd.

Suddenly that ghastly Bob pushed through, brandishing his banjo.

"That's all right, sergeant," he cried cheerfully; "this gentleman is a friend of mine."

The policeman's hair almost stood on end, and he lost the power of speech.

"Nothing of the kind," I protested; "I don't call a man my friend that goes about with a bucket on his head."

And the two of us started on a hot round of recriminations.

"Why can't I wear a high hat if I like?" cried Bob; "it's a healthy one, look at the ventilation."

He took it off, and showed us that the bottom had been knocked out.

"Well, why do you follow me about?" I shouted angrily.

"Why!" cried Bob, turning to the crowd with an appealing gesture, "he asks me why. Ah——, what would poor Mary say if she could see him now reproaching her only father?"

He turned his eyes heavenwards and wound up his clock.

"What are you talking about?" I said; "you had your share of the club money after the funeral expenses, and I had to do all the dirty work."

The crowd began to take a serious view of the
affair.

"'Pears to me," said the policeman, "there's been
some tragedy. You'd better come quietly with me."

But fortunately Bob's alarm clock just went off;
and, as if they thought it was an infernal machine,
the policeman and the crowd shrank back. In a
moment Bob and I seized our opportunity, and
shot away as fast as our legs could carry us.

After turning three corners we saw a cab standing and we jumped in, giving the driver half a crown,
and telling him to drive us to Coventry Street.

Bob had had to throw his bucket away while
running, and I don't think he was sorry.

"It was the one point of my costume that
might have been improved," he said.

Getting out of the cab we strolled down to the
pit door of the Prince of Wales's, and gave the
people fits. Bob sang a pathetic serenade called
"Meet me by the village inn when it's closing
time," and put such passionate expression into his
lines that his corset dropped off just as he finished.

However, he used it to go round and collect
the pennies in, and perhaps it was done on purpose,
seeing that he wore underneath a scarlet shirt with
the letters "S. A." on it.

I don't suppose a wandering nigger minstrel
ever had such a heavy collection. And when it
was over he turned round and said loftily:

"Ladies and gentlemen, I do this from a love
of art, not for gain," and walked down the row,

H.R.H., TO "VARIETY" HIGH LIGHTS: "YOU HAVE BEEN DOING SUCH WONDERS LATELY AT THE MUSIC-HALLS, THAT I MUST TRY TO ARRANGE A PERFORMANCE AT WINDSOR."

giving the pennies back to the people who had not given them, causing general joy and indignation according to circumstances.

Then he looked round for me, but I wasn't there. I was round the next corner.

You see it was not long before I was about to set off for my trip to the United States, and I felt that for a Plenipotentiary Extraordinary to conduct himself in that manner was probably without precedent in the diplomatic service.

*   *   *   *   *

My visit to America was, I consider, the crown of my career, for an English artiste does not as a rule go across the Atlantic until he has made a first-rate reputation in London.

With some assistance from Lord Salisbury and Mr. Chamberlain I have succeeded in bringing about a kindlier understanding between English and Americans.

WILLIAM BRENDON & SON, PLYMOUTH

CPSIA information can be obtained at www.ICGtesting.com
Printed in the USA
LVOW01s2016050614

388791LV00029B/1456/P